In the tradition of *Barbarians at the Gate* and *Den of Thieves*, Scott Brown's *Out of the Valley* is a true and revealing story of life at the top in corporate America. It is also a riveting account how F. Scott Brown, an honest and dedicated president of an international corporation, went to federal prison as a result of perjured testimony. Only then did he learn from a fellow prisoner of the existence of a half-century old international cartel, and how he had been framed by the cartel's leadership and then prosecuted by an overzealous Department of Justice as a scapegoat for the cartel's many years of violating U.S. antitrust laws. During his long ordeal, and throughout his subsequent efforts to reclaim his distinguished reputation, Scott Brown was sustained by his strong faith in God, by the strength and faith of his distraught family, and by his incredible network of steadfast, God-fearing friends and business associates throughout the country. Look for another book by Scott if the presently pending extradition and U.S. trial of Morgan Crucible's former CEO is ever approved by Britain's House of Lords.

—TYLER DEDMAN
REAR ADMIRAL
US NAVY, RETIRED

Saturday mornings, Scott Brown—former CEO and member of my businessmen's Bible study—comes to my home after feeding one hundred or so homeless men. His philanthropy is legendary. But, he took on a cartel, was betrayed, became the patsy, and was forced to accept federal confinement on a plea bargain. First bitter over damage to his reputation, Scott's book mirrors what I witnessed firsthand—the painful catharsis of his soul. *Out of the Valley* will touch your soul, too.

—DON BJORK, MINISTER IN RETIREMENT
HEATHROW, FLORIDA

OUT OF THE
VALLEY

OUT OF THE
VALLEY

F. SCOTT BROWN

CREATION
HOUSE
A STRANG COMPANY

OUT OF THE VALLEY by F. Scott Brown
Published by Creation House
A Strang Company
600 Rinehart Road
Lake Mary, Florida 32746
www.creationhouse.com

Unless otherwise noted, all Scripture quotations are from the Holy Bible, New International Version of the Bible. Copyright © 1973, 1978, 1984, International Bible Society. Used by permission.

Scripture quotations marked NKJV are from the New King James Version of the Bible. Copyright © 1979, 1980, 1982 by Thomas Nelson, Inc., publishers. Used by permission.

AUTHOR'S NOTE: STATEMENTS MADE HEREIN, INCLUDING THE RECOUNTING OF COURTROOM SCENES, ARE BASED ON EVIDENCE ON FILE AND IN THE POSSESSION OF THE AUTHOR.

Design Director: Bill Johnson
Cover design by Karen Grindley

Library of Congress Control Number: 2008939235
International Standard Book Number: 978-1-59979-532-4

First Edition

08 09 10 11 12—9 8 7 6 5 4 3 2 1
Printed in the United States of America

DEDICATION

O Lord, you took up my case; you redeemed my life. You have
seen, O LORD, the wrong done to me. Uphold my cause!
—LAMENTATIONS 3:58–59

FIRST AND MOST IMPORTANTLY, I DEDICATE MY LIFE TO MY LORD and Savior Jesus Christ and His work of helping the less fortunate. I dedicate this book:

To my wife Candy, whose love for me and faithful witness to God have made me the man I am today.

To our three children Meredith, Christine, and Rick, who were a constant source of love and unwavering trust and confidence. Mere words are insufficient to express my love, gratitude, and respect for these amazing individuals.

To J. David Quinn, my mentor, confidant, and friend. Dave was instrumental in developing me as a manager and instilling in me the importance of customer service, a competitive spirit, analytical skills, and leadership qualities necessary for success in today's global marketplace. Many thanks for walking alongside me every step of the way during this long and arduous journey.

To the former employees of the Pure Carbon Company and today's employees of Morgan AM&T (Advanced Materials and Technology). For your dedication, commitment, and loyalty throughout the years, I thank you. Your support touched my heart and my family in so many ways. I pray your greatest days as a company are still ahead of you and that you enjoy the fruits of your hard work.

To my pastor, the Rev. Charles Holt, his assistant, the Rev. Robert Mountford, and to all my brothers and sisters in Christ at St. Peter's

Episcopal Church in Lake Mary, Florida, who covered my family and me in unceasing prayer.

To Alan and Sharon Norris for their compassion and countless hours of listening to me when talking seemed like a balm for the mind and body. Thank you for your friendship and for your care and support of Candy while I was serving my sentence.

To my former pastor in St. Marys, Pennsylvania, the Rev. David Vaughn and my lifelong friend Roy Mills. Thank you for your steadfast encouragement and support. I am blessed to call you both true friends.

To my friend Bill Dillard, CEO of MSI, Orlando, Florida. Thank you for your encouragement and assistance in revitalizing my business career as a consultant. You have restored my dignity.

CONTENTS

ACKNOWLEDGMENTS

I WANT TO EXPRESS MY PERSONAL GRATITUDE AND SINCERE THANKS to the following people for their time, thoughts, suggestions, and encouragement during the process of developing the manuscript:

Barbara Trombitas, for your creative ideas and suggestions, the countless retypes, and your help with the readability of the book.

Rear Admiral Ty Dedman (U.S. Navy, retired) for your painstaking critique of the manuscript, identifying the areas requiring more clarity and substance, and your encouragement directed at enhancing the Lord's story throughout the manuscript.

Bobbi Vogel, a family friend and retired educator, who used her expertise to promote better sentence structure, understanding, and a people-friendly read.

James "Mac" McWhorter (Lt. Col. U.S. Army, retired), with whom I serve at the Grace-n-Grits ministry of Sanford, Florida, and who was instrumental in developing the structure of the book.*

Jim Younger, of Younger and Associates, for his detailed interviews of key people in my case. His professionalism and dedication in this process was most helpful to me in writing this book.

*My friend Mac McWhorter was called home to be with the Lord on Wednesday, October 22, 2008. Mac was a man of honor. He served our Lord Jesus, his family, and his country with the quiet dignity of a patriot. I am a better man for having known the blessing to have been called his friend.

FOREWORD

Good is the enemy of Great.[1]

ONSIDER THE OPERATIVE WORD OF THAT PHRASE COINED BY Jim Collins in the opening sentence of his book *Good to Great—enemy*. On one level, this book, *Out of the Valley*, is about how a great leader, by pursuing greatness for his company, became the fall guy for that very company and the target of the country he loves. On a deeper level, the book is about how God works all things for the good of those who love Him and are called according to His purpose—how true greatness from God's perspective does not always equal success in the worldly point of view.

I know Scott Brown as his pastor and as one of my parishioners. Such a relationship is sacred. As a pastor, I am often invited behind the scenes in a person's life into their soul's life. No human being can ever really know the soul of another human being. Only God has such knowledge. But my honor and privilege has been to glimpse a measure of the spiritual life of Scott Brown and his family and to walk with them in the journey of faith and frustration that occasioned the writing of this book.

Scott is a reformer to the core of his being. His primary gifting from God is to take that which is broken, mired in mediocrity, or even merely good, and transform it into something truly great. Jim Collins talks about the unique individuals among us who exhibit a quality of leadership that can move an organization, system, business, or whatever from mediocrity to greatness. Collins calls these leaders "level five leaders."[2] He describes these unusual individuals as those leaders who "build enduring greatness through a paradoxical blend of personal humility and professional will."[3]

Whether we are talking about the building of a global corporation or a local church summer camp for kids, Scott Brown has demonstrated level-five qualities at his core.

In order to reform any organization, whether you are talking about a church or a business, the reformer must have a steel will to persevere. In my circles, it is called faith—faith to see what should be and have perseverance to see it realized in the face of opposition. Over his career, Scott has shown a steel drive to see the carbon manufacturing business be great.

Many pundits have sounded the death knell on manufacturing in the United States. To be honest, manufacturing as a business sector in our nation has fallen on hard times. Some suggest that it is no longer possible for Americans to compete in a global market. They readily surrender the industry to cheaper labor costs of overseas plants and businesses.

But not Scott Brown! In example after example, he has demonstrated that with the right leadership, inspiration, and hard work, a U.S. manufacturing plant not only can be successful, but dominate the global marketplace. The secret is not only "steel will," but the added characteristic of deep humility and love for people.

As you read this book, you will hear humility as Scott gives credit for his success to his mentors and co-workers, God's providence, and fortunate circumstances. His employees love him, not only because he believed in their capabilities, but because he stepped into the trenches with them; down and dirty on the shop floor rather than remaining sequestered in a lofty office. He demonstrated by example what it means to work hard and care about giving your all for the sake of building something great.

But not every effort to reform is met with welcome arms. Scott would learn the meaning of sabotage and pain. Sometimes the forces that the reformer is seeking to change are more powerful (at least from a worldly point of view) than the reformer himself.

Such was the case when Scott became the global president of Morgan AM&T. He carried himself as the same corporate reformer that he had always been—his character of integrity, hard work, and faith did not waiver. He went right to work seeking to make the business more competitive and more efficient in Europe by building the right team, restructuring, and clearing dead weight.

As Scott began his work as the global president, he met one of the most formidable challenges of his life. Behind the scenes of his last corporate endeavor lay an unrevealed system that refused to be reformed: the European carbon cartel. Ironically, Morgan Crucible would become a *crucible* indeed, testing and proving the character of Scott Brown to the core.

We live in a world of human systems, whether we are talking about a family, business, government, or a congregation. Humans organize and develop systemic patterns within human relationships. These systems of relationships can be healthy and great, or they can be sick and dysfunctional. The reformer's high calling is to take sick human systems and make them healthy and highly functional. When it works, nothing is more rewarding or more fulfilling, not only for the reformer, but also for the many people liberated and enriched by the reforms.

When a human system is unhealthy, broken, and mired in mediocrity, there is usually a reason. Human sin and corruption are often present at the heart of the matter. It does not take long for a corrupted system to either seek to corrupt its reformer, or, if not possible, to eliminate him. This is why the work of reform is not for the faint of heart. It requires courage and will.

Recently I read a book called *The Shack* that is about a personal reform project of the life of one man. In a very perceptive and profound reaction, the God character in the book, Papa, reflects on corruption in human systems within creation: "Creation has been taken down a very different path than we desired. In your world the value of the individual is constantly weighed against the survival of the system, whether political, economic, social, or religious—any system actually. First one person, and then a few, and finally many are easily sacrificed for the good and the ongoing existence of that system. In one form or another, this lies behind every struggle for power, every prejudice, every war, and every abuse of relationship. The 'will to power and independence' has become so ubiquitous that it is now considered normal."[4]

The history of the people of God is littered with the martyrdom of great men and women who saw a better future for their people or human systems under their concern and yet found themselves thrown under the bus by the very people they were seeking to help. One such biblical figure was the first deacon of the church, Stephen. He asked his people who were stoning him, "Which of the prophets did you not stone?" (Acts 7:52).

Thank God there are people of integrity who take a stand for what is right and do the right thing in every sphere of society. Such people are the great lights of the world. Unfortunately, history betrays and reveals our true nature with respect to such heroes of the faith and reformers of society; far too often they are deeply wounded and often destroyed by the human systems they have ordained to reform.

In order to reform mediocrity, one must be willing to stand with a stern will; but even the strongest of wills cannot carry a body through the fires of persecution or the assassin's bullet. Sometimes in this "world of devils filled,"[5] evil seems to triumph over good.

Alas, the reformer's work to break the forces against change is well met. Sometimes the forces of corruption resist, and so the reformer is broken instead. Which of the prophets did you not stone?

One could ask whether living as such a person is worth the personal sacrifice and whether it makes any difference. Many have chosen the path of building something new rather than fixing something old. Is it worth it? On one level, the answer is no. The systems of the world have been, and will continue to be, corrupt. Even that which is repaired will one day be broken again. All labor is toil.

Is it worth it? From another perspective, the answer is a resounding yes. We never see the big picture—how God will use our efforts to accomplish His purposes. While from one side we may not accomplish "success," our brokenness may serve to further God's plan in some unknown way. This has been the history of redemption through the ages.

We also never know who will be inspired by our stand; we are always being watched by those around us. We should never underestimate the power of a leader who is upright and walks with integrity to inspire others to do the same. In Christian terms we call it our witness. Scott has been a witness to truth, patriotism, good business practices, greatness, and to Christian faith.

While for Scott this witness has been costly in ways none of us will ever be able to fully relate to financially, relationally, physically, or spiritually, his witness has not gone unnoticed by those who know Scott Brown. Those of us who have journeyed alongside him through his trials and faith are inspired. Those who have been responsible for his trouble have been humbled by his unusual ministry toward them. Government prosecutors, judges, and attorneys have acknowledged his character of integrity. But most importantly, Scott's sacrifices and faith have not gone unnoticed by God.

Whatever the worldly outcome, the Lord knows the attitudes of our heart. He is the One who sees in secret. He will reward those who earnestly seek Him.

Vindication in this life for the righteous is a fleeting thing. Even if it comes, ultimately it is unsatisfying and inadequate: "'Vengeance is Mine, I will repay,' says the Lord" (Rom. 12:19, NKJV). There is comfort in the knowledge that it is God's sovereignty to deal with injustice. Such understanding and wisdom enables the victim of injustice to move on with life comforted by the peace and grace of God. Such wisdom allows us to pray for the enemies that persecute us, even while remaining in relationship with them. It allows us to show them mercy and grace in their hour of need, even though they ruined us. This unusual behavior is the unique mark of the Christian life, the mark of a disciple who has picked up his cross and followed Jesus.

Those captivated by the ways of the world may never understand such behavior. Enemies who receive the grace of those whom they have persecuted often perceive it in negative terms, "heap[ing] burning coals on [the] head" (Prov. 25:22). Worldly-minded people may consider it foolishness. But for those who are being saved, such a witness is the wisdom and power of God. Through the crucified life, life is redeemed and changed for God. Scott has modeled this manner of life as a disciple of the Lord. The crucible is not something anyone would look for—it finds us because we follow the crucified One.

The Lord is pleased to use us most powerfully not in our successes, but in our failures; not in our victories and vindications, but through our persecutions and losses. The cross of Jesus Christ lies at the heart of the plan of God's salvation for those corrupted and destroyed by the systems of our fallen world.

—THE REV. CHARLES L. HOLT
RECTOR, ST. PETER'S EPISCOPAL CHURCH
LAKE MARY, FLORIDA

PREFACE

A VERY GOOD FRIEND OF MINE, PAUL BRUNO, PRESIDENT OF A performance management and training company, and his wife, Susie, an Episcopal deacon, helped me as dear friends and spiritual mentors to get through the most difficult time of my life. I was accused of violating federal antitrust laws—participating in an international carbon cartel. After an arduous three-year fight, I pleaded guilty in order to spare my family further torment. The six months I spent in prison were a near relief after struggling fruitlessly to clear my name—I never fixed prices, conspired to destroy documents, or plotted against the U.S. government to cover up those activities. But people in the company I worked for did. Somehow, which I will try to explain in this book, I became a fall guy for many others who were party to alleged cartel acts, but received immunity from prosecution.

At the start of my incredible legal journey, Paul wrote me a letter and said he was "deeply saddened by the critical and negative rhetoric that permeates this nation's discourse." He was hoping to witness an example of how our legal system can still function in a manner consistent with an underlying principle: as a citizen of the United States, an individual is presumed innocent until proven guilty.

Paul's words resonated with me throughout my battle. In a single day, I went from being a hard-working, law-abiding, tax-paying, proud American to a target of a criminal investigation into price fixing of carbon components in the United States. It was so stunning that it took me many months, even years, to unravel all the accusations against me—false accusations—and understand how on earth I was wrapped up in a case that reached across Europe, resulted in millions of dollars in fines, and set international legal precedent.

Paul's hope was that of every American: that our judicial system blindly weighs facts and delivers fair verdicts. My case was a grave disappointment, to say the least.

My story is also about God's mercy. I wish I could say that there are many valuable business lessons buried within my experience, but the truth is I did everything according to the book when it came to my career. I wasn't perfect, of course, but I tried to learn from my mistakes. I loved my job(s), and worked very hard to make my way up the corporate ladder. So, what do we do when, despite our best efforts, the world seems to conspire against us? That's a question everyone should ask. Even if you're riding the perfect wave right now, if you don't have an answer, there's a very real possibility the world will win someday. I would never have made it through this challenge without my Lord and Savior walking beside me and upholding my family, helping me overcome the world.

Should I just accept my sentence and move on, even though I'm now labeled a "convicted felon," losing many rights and privileges, including the opportunity to coach sports and work with young people, which I'd done for many years? Wouldn't it be easier to simply make the most of a comfortable yet compromised life? Yes. Is that the right thing to do?

No.

> You prepare a table before me in the presence of my enemies. You anoint my head with oil; my cup overflows.
> —Psalm 23:5

I heard, read, and sang Psalm 23 dozens of times in my life, but never really appreciated the part about being anointed by God in the midst of enemies. A descent can happen fast, unexpectedly, and it usually pulls down our loved ones, too. We grope in the dark valley, but, even there, God prepares a table and fills our cups to overflowing so we can confront evil instead of fleeing. Amidst the frightening fog of hopelessness, anger, and doubt, God sets out a feast—it's hard to appreciate such a banquet when enemies are bearing down.

God's mercy didn't scoop me up to the mountaintop (not that I didn't ask), but His grace slowly walked me through the valley. I had to hang on, accept the cup and drink, and find courage, knowing that God was with me.

I was in prison when I learned facts that corroborated my defense argument and supported my innocence. I found myself incarcerated with a key witness in my case who backed my version of events and supplied information I never knew. After more than three years of torment, much of it at the hands of my own government, I was crawling out of the darkness. God blessed me with more revelations after I was released. Mankind's imperfect judicial system brought me down, but the perfect Judge lifted me up.

For my children and grandchildren, for friends and colleagues, for every American, and for God's glory, I could not and did not flee—and now I must give my full account of what happened in the valley.

—F. SCOTT BROWN

Chapter 1
HIGHWAYS AND OPPORTUNITIES

W HEN YOU ARE TRAVELING NEARLY EVERY WEEK, SOMETIMES away for as long as a month, working sixteen-hour days, spending hours on long-range business plans, revitalizing sluggish productivity, and handling personnel issues, it's hard to imagine retiring. I wasn't planning on this rite of passage at age sixty-two, but after a very successful career in the carbon manufacturing industry, circumstances forced my hand.

I made the most of my new lifestyle. My wife, Candy, and I live near Orlando, Florida, in a beautiful golf community. We were very active in our church, and our children and grandchildren lived nearby. I still had one foot in consulting and investing opportunities, so for me, it was the best of both worlds.

Until one August afternoon in 2001.

After lunch and a pleasant swim with Candy and my son, Rick, I went in the house to change clothes. I was surprised to see a man in a business suit at my front door, especially since we live in a gated subdivision. He was an FBI agent, and he had a grand jury subpoena for me. I had never been in trouble with the law in my life, but that subpoena unleashed a chain of events that would send me to federal prison for six months because of activities within the British conglomerate Morgan Crucible, the company I worked for during my last five years of employment. I'd eventually find out that Morgan Crucible had been involved in a worldwide cartel for many years, and as a result of false accusations and leniency deals, I was wrongfully punished for participating.

I never could have imagined the tangled web of accusations and frustrating legal wrangling I was about to face. I knew the company was misguided when I asked for early retirement; that's why I left, but I was never aware of any illegal antitrust activity. I knew something was wrong, but I couldn't figure out what it was.

Retirement was over, and three years of torment began.

* * *

Thirty years ago, still youthful and armed with a business degree, I tested the waters at a few companies involved in the aerospace industry. Following the moon landing in July 1969, the early seventies was a thrilling time to be involved in the space program. I worked for ILC Industries at the National Aeronautics and Space Administration in Houston. ILC manufactured spacesuits for the Apollo Program, and I frequently interacted with the astronauts. Those years were also personally exciting because I often visited our manufacturing plant in Dover, Delaware, where I met Candy, my wife. A long-distance courtship evolved, but soon the phone bills and time apart made us miserable (there were no unlimited minutes back then.)

We married within a year. God truly blessed my life by bringing us together—for better or worse, she has been deeply committed to our family and me. The source of her strength is her Christian faith, which she helped me cultivate in my own life. After we were married, Candy moved to Texas and took a dream job working for the director of the Space Shuttle Program. It was the first of eleven moves she would make to support my career. Candy jokes that our family logged more moves than her brother during his career in the military.

By 1974 I'd been transferred to Delaware, but rumors circulated that my employer was going to be sold and relocated to Kansas City, Missouri, so I decided it was time for a career change. I replied to an ad for a job opportunity at Pure Carbon Company in St. Marys, Pennsylvania. I had never heard of the company or the city, and, to be honest, wasn't sure what carbon graphite manufacturing was all about, except maybe it had to do with pencils. However, the job was a supervisory position in quality control, a key function in a component manufacturing company, and also had an opportunity to move into an important sales position.

Driving six hours along frosty fields and icy roads to my interview, I realized part of my deliberating had to do with whether or not Candy and I wanted to commit to several more years of brutal winters. The landscape and beauty of rural Pennsylvania is remarkable, but St. Marys is near Lake Erie, an area referred to as the icebox of Pennsylvania.

The region is also rich in history, including the evolution of the carbon graphite industry, which emerged in the late 1800s with growing demand for dry cell batteries (not pencils). Carbon is an excellent conductor of electricity, and there are thousands of uses for carbon products. The automotive industry is a key consumer of electrical carbon brushes, and they're also found in household items such as power tools, air conditioners, kitchen appliances, and vacuum cleaners. Electrical current collectors keep mass transit rail trains running. Mechanical carbon and graphite products, which are primarily seals and bearings, can withstand high friction, are chemically non-reactive, and have self-lubricating properties. Pressed and machined carbon parts are used in everything from handheld kitchen mixers to atomic submarines.

In 1906, the parent company of Pure Carbon, Stackpole Corporation, formed under the name Stackpole Battery Company. St. Marys became known as the carbon capital of the world, and by 1992, twenty-four carbon graphite and powder metal companies could trace their roots back to Stackpole.

I went through a series of interviews at Pure Carbon and took tests for mechanical aptitude, a personality profile, and the Wonderlic Personnel test, designed to measure intelligence. Obviously the company was thorough. My final interview was with the president of the Pure Carbon Company, Dave Quinn. After a tense morning of interview jitters, Quinn settled me down. He moved from his desk to sit next to me, and asked about my family, where I grew up (we were both from West Virginia), and my long-term aspirations. He seemed genuinely interested and concerned for my family and the decision I would make regarding the position, if offered. I wasn't wrong in my assessment that day—Dave Quinn became my mentor and remains a special, loyal, and lifelong friend.

I left St. Marys feeling confident about my prospects, but not sure how to respond if an offer came through. Actually, the first time Pure Carbon called to arrange another interview, I respectfully turned them down. We had just had our first child, Meredith, and my in-laws lived nearby, so it didn't seem like a good time to uproot. Fortunately, Pure Carbon called again, and Candy said she wanted to see the area for herself.

This time I was taken to the plant in Coudersport, Pennsylvania, a community of slightly more than two thousand residents. The facility there had grown over the years to two hundred forty thousand square feet situated on sixty acres. It was the premier mechanical carbon plant in the world, but there were problem areas that needed to be addressed, and with my background in quality control, I saw this as a great career opportunity. Candy actually encouraged me to accept the position, and in 1974 I began my career in carbon manufacturing.

We soon adjusted to the atmosphere of a very small town. Candy was amazed, and a little horrified, that it really did snow every day for months, as people had warned. We had also left a brand new house in Delaware and ended up in a sixty-year-old home with drafts, creaks, and about ten layers of wallpaper; but Candy rallied, and we fondly recall the joy and occasional unsteadiness of starting a family in a strange town. Having left the comfort and security of her parents living a short drive away, we were blessed to have an older couple next door that "adopted" us and doted on two-year-old Meredith.

We were only in Coudersport for about one year, but during that time I successfully implemented a quality control procedure that reduced the amount of scrap produced in the manufacturing process from 24 percent to less than 5 percent. The accomplishments were lauded in the upper ranks of the company, but I owed a lot of credit to two of the best supervisors I've ever worked with, Joe Faust and Audrey Sullivan, and to a dedicated workforce.

My quality control success at Coudersport caught Dave Quinn's attention. Relatively new to the company, I had at least figured out he was *the* man at Pure Carbon, the one whose attention was both coveted and feared. He offered me the position of corporate quality assurance manager, with the added incentive that in time I could possibly move into sales and marketing. I was pursuing my MBA at that time, and my thesis was "The Development of a Marketing Support Program for New Industrial Products." Despite a peer's friendly warning about working directly for Quinn—a tough boss—I couldn't pass up the offer. Following the birth of our second daughter, Christine, Candy and I moved the family to St. Marys.

Dave Quinn gave me the opportunity to break into sales, and I traveled with Pure Carbon's top salespeople to meet customers and see firsthand how our products were used. My first success was landing the Johnson Corporation account in Three Rivers, Michigan. I had been paired with Tony Massaro, a talented application engineer, and we made dozens of trips to the facility before winning the business. Massaro played a key role in jump-starting my career—and he would also play a significant role in ending it.

While I was getting my feet wet learning the carbon business, Dave Quinn, a true visionary, was on the lookout for new business opportunities. At his direction, Pure Carbon acquired Syntax Corporation in Bay City, Michigan, in an effort to adapt silicon carbide conversion technology to Pure Carbon's expanding seal and bearing businesses. But there was a friction problem at Syntax, and it had nothing to do with our products. Terms of the acquisition included multi-year contracts for the three original owners, but they resented having their technology transferred to Pure Carbon and progress at the plant stagnated. From the start, there were many missed opportunities in the semiconductor and chemical processing markets because of the discord.

Dave Quinn invited me to visit Syntax with him on several occasions, and I was essentially a silent observer in a series of frustrating meetings trying to uncover why the business wasn't moving forward. After my quality control success at Coudersport, Quinn eventually offered me the position of vice president and general manager of Syntax. Working on site was the only way to make headway, and, quite honestly, I was becoming known as "Dave's boy" at the company; I had to prove I could independently handle an assignment like Syntax. Even though we'd just poured the foundation of a new home, Candy supported my decision, and I told Quinn I wanted to start immediately. I was in Michigan the following Monday, and Candy and the kids soon followed.

It didn't take long to figure out what was wrong. I arrived at seven o'clock, and the first employee arrived three hours later. The management didn't make it until noon. "Fresh meat," one yelled. "We'll run you out like all the others," another said. I laughed and instructed the workforce to gather for a brief meeting. The "three amigos" left for lunch and never returned that day.

We started with basics. The plant was in total disarray, so a few people went to the local hardware store for chemicals to strip and seal the floor, and we cleaned, painted, and repaired damaged walls. It was a long day, and at the end, I had the founders' three desks placed against a back wall, one in each corner and one in the middle. As expected, they wanted to see me the next day.

"We have contracts," they announced.

"Yes, you do," I said, "and you will honor them. I'm going to clean up this rats' nest and start servicing customers. You can join in or you can sit at your desks for eight hours a day. It's up to you."

For a month the three sat and did nothing from 8 a.m. until 4 p.m. while I familiarized myself with the plant equipment and got the rest of the crew back on track. Eventually they grew tired of watching the transformation from the sidelines. The first of the malcontents stepped up and said he wanted back in the game. He had been the sales manager and had a great track record in the industry, and the other two soon followed—Syntax began its turnaround.

Prior to working at Syntax, I had limited exposure to monthly profit and loss statements, yearly budgets, or five-year business plans, but I got a crash course at "Quinn University." I had my shortcomings on the financial side of the business prior to that, but working for Quinn galvanized my knowledge and analytical skills in this area. Syntax had a steady uphill climb toward commendable growth and earnings during my eighteen-month tenure, and I attribute our success to the team's ability to come together and focus on customer service.

In December 1976, Quinn offered me the job of sales manager of the Pure Carbon Company back in St. Marys, reporting to John Clark. I readily accepted the job because Pure Carbon was where I wanted to work. I loved the sales side of the business, and learning from Clark was a great opportunity. Ninety days into the job, Quinn called me in to review a series of sales calls I'd completed on the West Coast, which we discussed for nearly two hours, and then he changed the subject to the Tribon Bearing Company. Over the years I learned to pay very close attention to the *last* topic Quinn brought up in a meeting. The Tribon Bearing Division of Pure Industries was Quinn's brainchild. He saw an opportunity to develop new business by moving the manufacturing of selected aircraft components from St. Marys to a new plant in Cleveland, Ohio. He saw this market moving toward state-of-art materials such as polymides to reduce engine weight and enhance performance. The product primarily sold to aircraft engine manufacturers and sub-assemblers servicing the aerospace market. Quinn wanted me to move to Cleveland and concentrate my time and talents on jump-starting our operations, which had lost focus and momentum during the relocation. I accepted the challenge, and in 1977 the Brown family, now numbering five with our newborn son, Rick, moved to Strongsville, Ohio.

Candy again uprooted the kids from schools and doctors, and it was important to us to find a church. It was sometimes difficult to build a network of friends during the brief stints we had in different locations, but Candy had a positive attitude and deep faith that God watched over us.

"I took marriage vows to love and support you," she said. "I want to be home with the kids, so we're blessed that I'm able to do that. I just look at each move as an adventure."

In Cleveland I reported to John Thorp at Tribon Bearing Company. He was the former owner and president of Airborne Manufacturing in Elyria, Ohio, before selling his company and joining Tribon as its president. My relationship with Thorp started out a bit rocky, but I developed great respect for him as both a business leader and visionary during the twelve months I worked at Tribon.

Once again, though, I didn't get too comfortable in my new assignment—Quinn presented me the opportunity to return to Pure Carbon Company as vice president of operations in 1980, reporting directly to him. Thorp encouraged me to stay at Tribon, which had turned the corner operationally and profitably, but my love for Pure Carbon was the deciding factor. I also looked forward to working directly for Quinn again—there was always something to learn from him. My path seemed to keep leading me back to Pure Carbon, and this wasn't the last time I'd make the move.

During the next two years, I lived the Pure Carbon Company experience. I went to work early and stayed late every day, seven days a week. I reserved Sunday mornings and afternoons for my family and church, but by late afternoon I was usually focused on customer service issues, sales opportunities, or preparing for a business trip. I was consumed with passion and determination to be on top of every operational issue and business opportunity. I exhausted myself with micromanagement while pushing for broad, ambitious goals.

Looking back, I know my life was out of balance and included several misplaced priorities, but I lacked perspective to put things in order. I worked so furiously to get where I was, I wasn't sure where to go from there. I felt lost and empty and lacked a sense of personal accomplishment.

Overstressed and under motivated, I made the poor decision to leave Pure Carbon in 1981 to work for Wickes Engineered Materials in Saginaw, Michigan. Wickes experienced some rocky times, and at one point I had the opportunity to return to Pure Carbon, but pride made me stick it out to prove I could make it somewhere else. I did what I could at Wickes, but when the company announced the Carbon Division was for sale, I took a job as vice president of marketing and sales for Metalized Carbon Corporation in Ossining, New York. For six years, 1981 to 1987, I competed directly with Pure Carbon. I would run into former co-workers from time to time on the road, and we worked diligently but honestly to outdo one another. I never spoke with Quinn during that time.

Metalized Carbon eventually bought out my contract in an effort to downsize, and I decided it was time to try my own business. I had contacts in Florida, and Candy and I were ready for some sunshine, so in 1987, my family moved near Orlando, where I established Southeast Marketing and Sales. My focus was bearings and seals used primarily in pulp and paper mills, and I needed the best carbon materials available.

I contacted an old friend at Pure Carbon, Floyd Gerber, and ended up purchasing nearly a quarter million dollars in materials annually from Pure Carbon. At one point, though, the prices nearly tripled, and Gerber said he had no control over the increase. About this time Dave Quinn called with news that a mutual friend had passed away. It was good to talk to him, and I took the opportunity to request a meeting about my carbon prices. Weeks later, I flew to St. Marys and met with him for the first time in seven years. He resolved the pricing issue and even invited me to Pure Carbon's sales meeting in the United Kingdom to present my product line. I thought, "This is a remarkable man." I competed against Pure Carbon for seven years, but he never held it against me or took it personally.

It wasn't long before Quinn called me again and asked to visit my operation in Florida. I was a little nervous at the thought of my former boss seeing my new venture. Candy and I had gone from one extreme to the other, from the icebox to the sauna. It was August, and the floor of my manufacturing facility wasn't air conditioned. I was a one-man operation, too, producing the products myself except for one part-time assistant. Candy took care of accounting. This was far from Quinn's world, but our business was lucrative, and he knew I had once again taken a product from beginning to end and had many satisfied customers in a niche market.

Quinn and I dripped sweat through the plant tour and then froze in my tiny office. He had more on his mind, though, and asked me to dinner to address the real reason for his visit.

"Scotty, we started together, let's end together," he said. "I'm going to retire soon, and I want to present you for consideration as my replacement."

It was hard to believe I once again had an opportunity to return to Pure Carbon, this time to replace Quinn as president. I would have to pass muster with Lyle Hall, chairman of the Stackpole Corporation, Pure Carbon's parent company, and Sam Parkhill, Stackpole's president, but I was honored that Quinn had that much confidence in me and respected the business decisions I'd made, even the one to leave Pure Carbon.

But this time the stakes really hit home. Candy was my partner at Southeast Marketing and Sales, handling all correspondence, quotes, and accounts payable. She dedicated herself to the company's success while holding down another full-time job at a realty firm, not to mention the demands of raising three children. Our business was debt-free, and we'd been profitable from the beginning. For nearly three years, we reinvested every penny back into the business. After moving nearly ten times, did we want to give up what we'd built to uproot our family again and return to corporate life? We'd developed a wonderful circle of friends, were well established in our church and active in various outreach ministries. I was assistant coach of a high school football program and loving it. If it had been any other company, I would have answered no in a heartbeat, but my roots ran deep at Pure Carbon. After a few meetings, and even more employment screening tests, Lyle Hall and Sam Parkhill approved the transition. I felt like I was going home when I returned to St. Marys in 1990 as president of Pure Carbon.

How often do we sit back and contemplate critical decisions in our lives and wonder whether it was God's will or our own that played out? Did my pride drive the course of events, or did I make a sound, wise decision, even though it brought dreadful consequences? Of course there were many times I thought about the decision to return to Pure Carbon and how different life would have been if I'd stayed in Florida. I certainly didn't do it for the money—we were far better off with our own business. There were years of professional gratification, but accepting that offer eventually brought immeasurable anguish and frustration upon my family and me. The experience also molded me into a more humble, prayerful man. I must believe that God knew what I ultimately needed and engineered my circumstances for His glory. With the benefits of age, an incredibly supportive wife and family, and valuable spiritual guidance, I realize the wisdom God had in store for me had nothing to do with productivity levels and customer service.

I now believe that God allowed me to return to Pure Carbon, knowing that the new position would pose major challenges, both professionally and spiritually. If I were unable to resolve these struggles, my career, my family, and even my very existence would be at risk. What I had to learn, and to accept, was that these challenges—and the resulting choices—would also strengthen me spiritually and prepare me to fulfill my responsibility as a Christian to carry out Christ's Great Commission. In short, the journey upon which I was embarking reflected God's plan for the rest of my life, both in a secular and spiritual sense.

Many are the plans in a man's heart, but it is the LORD's purpose that prevails.

—PROVERBS 19:21

Chapter 2
WHITE KNIGHT

T HE FIVE-PLUS YEARS I WORKED FOR STACKPOLE CORPORA-
tion as president of Pure Carbon were among the most rewarding
professionally in my life. I'd made it to the top of the company I loved.
Tremendous challenges greeted me, and I was excited about every opportunity. With the formation of Pure Industries in 1979, Dave Quinn had
less time to manage day-to-day activities of Pure Carbon as he focused
on emerging technologies at several new companies under the Pure
Industries banner. There were new operations in New Jersey, Tennessee,
Ohio, Michigan, Florida, and Pennsylvania. Like a neglected child, Pure
Carbon needed special attention.

Sam Parkhill, president of Stackpole, was my new boss. He liked the
Nike slogan "Just Do It," and had a positive attitude about slow but steady
progress. Sam understood fixing the problems would take time, but he
wanted to make sure we kept moving forward. Pure Carbon Company,
like most of Stackpole's business holdings, would eventually be sold,
although it would be one of the last to go.

My first major challenge came when the January 1990 financials were
published—despite major restructuring efforts in 1989, Pure Carbon
Company still lost more than three hundred thousand dollars during my
first month on the job. It was evident that the business volume wouldn't
support the overhead structure still in place. There were many sleepless
nights as I figured out how to cut fifty salaried positions, because it meant
letting top performers go. On the customer service side, our productivity,
delivery performance, and lead times were abysmal, but that would take
some time to fix.

Back at the Coudersport plant, where I started with Pure Carbon, union
organizers were responding to disgruntled hourly employees whose health
benefits were reduced. Management hadn't effectively communicated the

reason for the changes (skyrocketing premium costs), and morale bottomed out. This was a far cry from the family atmosphere I left in 1979.

On the home front, Candy reconnected with some friends, but our kids were older now and we also met new people through different sports and activities. Even though we'd lived there before, it was, as Candy said, another adventure to get resettled.

In a sense, I was back where I started twenty years earlier—finding ways to get Coudersport back on track. I spent my first eight weeks on the shop floor catching up on what had changed, unraveling the production schedule, and identifying bottlenecks. Walking the floor for sixteen hours a day also gave me the opportunity to talk at length with employees and explain in detail the rationale behind benefits changes. I also emphasized that we had to resolve our customer service issues as quickly as possible. I introduced the slogan "Customers First—Whatever it Takes," long before it was vogue. I made headway by calmly and logically explaining that jobs were on the line if performance didn't improve. The union issue also weighed us down, and it was time to let the employees choose. The outcome was close, but the union won. At least now we could focus on moving forward.

Roy Wilder was the president of the Coudersport union, and I give him a lot of credit for the attitude change and commitment to customer service it generated through the plant. When customers visited, Wilder often volunteered to be the tour guide; and in reality, he was one of our top salespeople due to his passion and enthusiasm. He became a major contributor to our success.

Sixteen-hour days in Coudersport with my colleague, Floyd Gerber, became routine. We left St. Marys every morning at four o'clock and returned around eight. I spent many nights asleep in a chair at the Pure Carbon Lodge. We decided to bring in consultants to help with our customer service issues, and chose a California firm, IMR. It was an excellent call; there was immediate synergy with Pure Carbon's management, but Gerber and I didn't hide behind the consultants—we were front-and-center for every change we made at the plant. Within about six months, an average of six hundred late orders was reduced to single digits, and customer lead times fell from roughly thirteen weeks to three.

After nine months, Pure Carbon once again reported positive financials. As profits rose, so did morale. Working on the shop floor during this time also allowed me to evaluate the energy and aptitude of individual supervisors who could keep the momentum going once I pulled back from my oversight role.

In 1990, midway through our project with IMR, Sam Parkhill told me that the French company, Carbone, had bought our electrical brush business. The news was a shock, and, as usually happens, waves of suspicion and job insecurity spread through the workforce. I had gained the trust of our employees at this point, and I convinced everyone I didn't have prior knowledge of the sale. However, this change now put our mechanical carbon business front and center and highlighted the fact that it was barely breaking even. I called an emergency meeting of our top manufacturing and engineering personnel to discuss remedies.

A young engineering department manager, Paul Schulz, had worked diligently to automate the electrical brush division, making it Pure Carbon's most profitable product line, and he brought the same energy and innovation to the mechanical carbon side of our business in the Coudersport plant. He and his team prepared a modernization program and made a dynamic presentation that would dramatically change the profitability, throughput, and quality of our carbon seal and bearing businesses. His proposal was to replace all the manual lathes in the Coudersport plant with state-of-the-art equipment, which would require significant capital investment because there were fifty-five small lathes in the seal machining area alone. The move would result in additional depreciation expense, and there was uncertainty over whether or not we could meet the forecasted return on investment. Schulz also detailed potential benefits of a set-up reduction program. These new ideas were intriguing, but our hurdle was selling them to Stackpole's president and my boss, Sam Parkhill.

The IMR project had cost Stackpole Corporation in excess of five hundred thousand dollars, but I believe its success gave us credibility with Parkhill, and he saw the passion and results coming from the workforce at Coudersport. In the months and years that followed, Stackpole Corporation invested several million dollars in new equipment to bolster Pure Carbon back to its position as a world-class manufacturing company.

Parkhill also introduced the Stackpole Standards of Excellence Program that included much of the same criteria as the better-known Malcolm Baldridge Award. The internal system gave management constructive ways to measure operational and financial progress, and its incentives motivated teams to strive for improvements. As Pure Carbon focused on initiatives to stay strong in the marketplace, I promoted and hired very capable talent because I wanted to focus more time on our European business, which was doing quite well in Great Britain, but had weak legs in the German and Scandinavian markets that had great potential for growth.

Midway through year two of my presidency at Pure Carbon, Peter Bloom's resume hit my desk. He was a young Harvard MBA graduate and already worked for Stackpole Canada. When I called for background information, Bloom's supervisor did not recommend him, but based on an impressive resume, I invited Bloom to come to St. Marys for an interview anyway. I felt he was someone who could keep our team moving toward peak performance. I was very pleased that Bloom accepted our employment offer and that his performance exceeded my expectations.

Those first few years back at Pure Carbon were exhausting but energizing. Long hours, difficult management decisions, expensive plant upgrades, union negotiations, and incentives to motivate the workforce paid off. By the end of the third quarter 1990, our customer service efforts began to pay dividends as on-time delivery performance, coupled with major reductions in lead time, took hold. During the next year or so our market share grew in the United States and profitability began a steady climb upward. However, on the downside, Stackpole Corporation continued to reduce its holdings, and by late 1993, Pure Carbon Company was positioned for a sale.

Shortly thereafter, Lyle Hall, chairman of Stackpole Corporation, asked me to join him in a series of meetings with prospective buyers for Pure Carbon in Japan and Europe. Morgan Crucible, a British conglomerate and a major competitor, emerged as the most interested. Morgan Crucible had previously acquired Carbon Technology, a mechanical carbon manufacturer based in Rhode Island, in an effort to gain market share in North America and re-establish their presence in the United States.

Negotiations dragged on for months. Curiously, there wasn't interest from other European carbon manufacturers like Carbone, SGL, or Schunk. Finally another British company with significant business in the United States, Turner and Newell, came on the scene. Within two months, Turner and Newell's acquisition team completed its due diligence and made an offer that was substantially more than Morgan Crucible had on the table, and Stackpole accepted.

It wasn't time to kick back, though. We had to maintain Pure Carbon's financial performance until the sale was final. In addition, I was heavily involved in discussions about the transition. The period was stressful and consuming for me and for the rest of the management team, and we looked forward to deferred vacations. I promised Candy a trip to Florida as soon as it was over.

On the morning of the scheduled closing, I called Turner and Newell and learned the deal was completed. I shared the news with my management team and then headed to Florida. As was customary, I left my travel itinerary with my secretary, and when I opened the door to my hotel room, the telephone light was flashing. The message was from Sam Parkhill. "He must want to congratulate me," I thought. When I called Parkhill's Boston office, he informed me that the sale had collapsed. Candy and I caught the next available flight back to Pennsylvania. Turner and Newell issued a press release stating that Turner and Newell had pending asbestos claims amounting to thirty or forty million dollars, which had just come to light, and for that reason, could not close the acquisition of the Pure Carbon Company.

How could a company invest so much time and expense into making an acquisition and discover on the day the deal was to close they had serious liability issues? It made no sense. I was perplexed and frustrated at the same time.

The fallout had us once again turning to Morgan Crucible. Parkhill was concerned we wouldn't be able to get Morgan back to the table. He then asked me if I thought I could get the chairman of Morgan Crucible's Carbon Division, Ian Norris, to restart the negotiating process. I said I could and proceeded to contact Norris. Norris was somewhat hesitant because he felt Parkhill had pulled the rug from under Morgan the last time. I assured him I would be his primary contact and Parkhill would only monitor the negotiations. Once again the deal was on.

Pure Carbon's profits had nearly doubled from fiscal 1993 to 1994, and we projected a staggering 60 percent increase in 1995 that was based, in part, on prospective new business. Morgan Crucible obviously downplayed the viability of a major prospective account, an automotive application for a lumbar seat pump. The bargaining continued, and even though the new automotive application never reached its full potential, we still exceeded the 60 percent profit increase we had forecasted.

Although Parkhill had said he would only monitor the negotiations, I received a last-minute call from him about another potential buyer. A New York investment firm, Value Added Capital, had contacted Parkhill because one of its employees had a relative who worked at the Coudersport plant. I spoke by phone with Value Added's representative, Bob Edgreen, and a week later he visited St. Marys with a very attractive proposal. The purchase offer not only exceeded Morgan Crucible's, it also included a stock option for me worth two and a half million dollars in the new company, and each member of my management team would receive five hundred thousand dollars in stock.

I called a meeting and presented Value Added's proposal to my team. Then I asked for a secret ballot on whether to go with Morgan Crucible or Value Added. I abstained. The vote was unanimous for Value Added.

That night, my brain told me the vote made the decision clear, but my heart wasn't convinced. "Sleep on it," Candy said. "You'll know what to do in the morning." She was right. Looking in the mirror while shaving the next morning, I realized the Value Added proposal was outstanding for my management team and me, but wrong for the rest of Pure Carbon's employees. Value Added would likely sell Pure Carbon again in three to five years, and that wasn't in the best interest of the people who devoted so much energy and time to the company. I told my colleagues the deal with Morgan Crucible was the best one for *all* our employees, and then informed Morgan Crucible that the wheels were in motion to finalize the deal. I would be integral in the transition and remain in management within the new hierarchy.

In the years ahead while employed at Morgan Crucible, my confusion over the failed Turner and Newell deal was justified when I heard allusions that Morgan Crucible blocked the deal, although I never learned exactly how. I also heard Ian Norris, who would become president of Morgan Crucible, and other executives say several times that acquiring Pure Carbon was one of the best decisions they ever made.

Choosing the Morgan Crucible offer was one of the worst decisions of my life, and the unimaginable price I paid wasn't merely lost stock options. I had no idea I was working for a company that was part of a carbon cartel in Europe, and the goal was to move it into the United States. Oh, the benefit of hindsight! I should have paid a lot more attention to those little red flags and illogical moves. I wondered why so few companies came forward to at least consider acquiring Pure Carbon and was shocked at Turner and Newell's last-minute withdrawal—but you don't know what you don't know, and I was operating in good faith.

Morgan Crucible's acquisition of Pure Carbon Company on March 15, 1995 wasn't well received by several of our key customers. The introduction of Morgan Advanced Materials and Technology (MAMAT), renamed Morgan AM&T within a year, raised concerns because Morgan Crucible had acquired three former competitors in the mechanical carbon manufacturing business: Pure Carbon, National Mechanical Carbon, and Carbon Technology. Now these three entities operated under the umbrella of Morgan AM&T, and our customers worried about the lack of competitive pricing and service. This was a sign of the times, though, and two of our major accounts, John Crane and Flowserve, had also moved to lock in their market positions by acquiring competitors. I worked with Morgan AM&T's global president, Roy Waldheger, previously president of Carbon Technology, to alleviate fears and assure customers that we were committed to customer service and effectively consolidating the corporation's research and development programs for even greater product quality.

That doesn't mean we were internally immune to the sniping and parochialism that often comes with merging competitors. As vice president and general manager of this newly formed company, I found myself refereeing one dispute after another. The infighting and accusations were reminiscent of my first few months back on the Coudersport shop floor. Waldheger seemed almost paranoid that Carbon Technology was out of favor, but it wasn't true. I finally established and chaired the Pricing Policy Board, and rules were clearly defined for all the business units to insure equity. The rancor dissolved over time, and Morgan AM&T's financial performance in the first year exceeded expectations.

In 1997, Bruce Farmer, president of Morgan Crucible, stepped down and became Chairman of the Board. Rumors flew about who would replace him: Nigel Howard or Ian Norris, both longtime Morgan Crucible employees, were the leading candidates. The two were highly intelligent, personable, and competitive. I saw it as a choice between Norris's ability to generate results or Howard's broader management experience. Norris, a thirty-year employee of Morgan Crucible, worked his way up from a systems analyst to tirelessly traveling the globe to expand the carbon business, and his worldwide group of companies was financially the best in Morgan Crucible's group. He was eventually tapped to replace Farmer, and while Howard's disappointment was apparent, he was a loyal soldier and carried on. After all, he and Norris were good friends.

Ian Norris had a reputation as a personnel theorist—he keenly recognized individual strengths and talent and plugged the right people into the right positions. His subordinates genuinely liked him and there was an intense loyalty among his closest allies and friends. We had several discussions before, during, and immediately after the acquisition, and he was upfront and fair. One issue we deliberated had to do with my retirement compensation. When I returned to Pure Carbon after nine years, Dave Quinn offered to add that time to my total years of service, but Sam Parkhill had concerns about federal employment regulations and never finalized the package. Norris took care of the problem by placing me in Morgan Crucible's Top Hat Retirement Program, essentially locking in those promised benefits.

During the transition, Norris and I also discussed hierarchy: I would report to Roy Waldheger, global president, and my new title would be vice president and general manager for Morgan AM&T–The Americas. (Norris worried that it might sound like a demotion, but I told him job titles were of little concern to me.) He said Pure Industries' businesses would be split into three distinct groups: the Americas, Europe, and Asia Pacific. He also mentioned the Pure Industries plant in Redditch, United

Kingdom, that previously reported to me but would fall under European management. I supported the decision to name Laurence Bryce, formerly my direct report for Pure Industries in Europe, as my counterpart at Morgan AM&T–Europe.

The worldwide restructuring made sense to me at the time, but it turned out to be a terrible mistake. In the first eighteen months, nearly four million dollars of business that Pure Carbon had established in Europe vanished. Customer sales calls plunged 70 percent. This situation was especially aggravating because prior to 1995, Pure Carbon spent considerable time and expense developing the European market and efforts paid off with steady growth. I had concentrated on customers in Germany and Denmark and discovered prices there for comparable materials were much higher than in the United States. I felt like all our past efforts and future opportunities were slipping away…fast! And I had lost direct control over managing the European marketplace.

Roy Waldheger invited me to attend a Morgan AM&T–Europe review meeting, and, to my surprise, I discovered there wasn't a board of directors or overview committee to monitor results like we had in the U.S.. Without a board or oversight committee, it seemed there weren't clear standards for my European counterparts. The situation was baffling. Laurence Bryce actually worked for Morgan Crucible early in his career, and then Dave Quinn hired him in the 1980s to work in research and development for Pure Carbon. Quinn later selected Bryce to spearhead the expansion of Pure Industries Limited in Europe. Bryce did well seeking out new business opportunities and capitalizing on areas where Morgan Crucible fell short with customers. After Morgan Crucible acquired Pure Carbon and restructured our management hierarchy, he suddenly seemed incapable of establishing any sales momentum, and I no longer had authority to hold him accountable.

I wrote two lengthy letters to Bryce and listed in detail my concerns about his team's support for our sales in Europe. In 1997, I told him we would no longer pay a fee for sales calls, but only commissions on business sold. Bryce also had a cumbersome system in place in which our quotations to European customers had to be reviewed by his sales manager, Edye Thein, to make sure we weren't undercutting Morgan

AM&T–Europe's prices. It was ludicrous because we were supposed to be on the same team—our results sure didn't show it.

My two letters were ineffective. Bryce countered by blaming the downfall on poor service from my end, which I documented was false. I figured that when I pulled the plug on paying nearly seven hundred dollars per sales call in Europe, my boss, Waldheger, would take notice and intercede in what I saw as a very serious situation, but nothing happened.

The nonproductive nature of this relationship also played out in dealings with the customer Borg Warner Industrial Products (BWIP). In 1996, Morgan AM&T–The Americas had forecasted nine hundred thousand dollars in sales to BWIP in the United States and more than two hundred thousand to their operations in Holland. Edye Thein sought Waldheger's help to try and convince me to significantly raise my prices on all parts sold to BWIP in order to match the price levels of Morgan AM&T–Europe. Waldheger forwarded me a compilation of European price data supplied by Thein, and I collected BWIP sales data for the United States from Floyd Gerber, then vice president of sales, and from Ken Huling, sales manager of Carbon Technology. I sent the price comparisons to Waldheger and noted, "It is quite obvious that the European prices are significantly higher than those in North America." Thein complained again to Waldheger that European sales to BWIP were down 31 percent, but we weren't reaping the windfall because our sales were down 42 percent at the time, and Huling's division had only a marginal increase. Then Waldheger asked about our sales margins, and I told him that was the key question. I had no idea what Europe's costs were, but I was happy with our margins and refused to change pricing. I never heard another word about BWIP.

I knew the acquisition would bring changes and headaches, but this was not my business style. I loved the heat of the marketplace—tug-of-war negotiations to win customers, the pressure to beat a competitor, and confronting and improving internal corporate conditions to build a successful organization and excel at customer service. I was not used to, or pleased about, spinning my wheels by volleying accusations with peers in my own company. I worked long and hard because I cared about the company, the people, and, yes, knowing I succeeded at my job. It was insufferable to watch the company I helped energize suddenly hobble along.

There was a lot at stake with another critical account, John Crane, the world's largest seal manufacturer and Morgan AM&T's biggest customer. Margins ran lower for John Crane, but the volume was roughly six million dollars a year. Sales decreased somewhat in 1995 because of cost control measures at John Crane, and Waldheger contacted me about maintaining and growing our carbon and silicon carbide sales. I knew we had to continue moving forward with our research and development efforts for selective materials to help solve John Crane's friction and wear issues, and our customer service had to be absolutely top notch. Sales executive Tony Massaro had handled this account for twenty-two years, and I recommended he continue to nurture the relationship.

Prior to a John Crane meeting in St. Marys in September 1996, I prepared a memorandum outlining our approach to maintaining and building the John Crane account. The key aspects were: delivery service at 95 percent initially and then achieving 99 percent by the year 2000; quality at 99 percent or better with all shipping locations certified; engineering services monthly; materials approval for all carbon and silicon carbide applications; cost reduction teams in place at major locations with defined goals for both companies; and a reduction in lead times.

The other significant piece of the plan was a simple business volume discount set to incrementally achieve a five-year mark of twelve million dollars in volume for a 5.5 percent discount. John Crane's purchasing manager at the time, Dan Kennedy, said he had approval for twelve million dollars with Pure Carbon in 1995. He also told us that purchases with other companies exceeded sixty million dollars, and those included carbon, silicon carbide, and tungsten carbide material components that Morgan AM&T was capable of supplying. I quickly relayed the potential opportunity to Waldheger, who passed it along to Ian Norris and Bruce Farmer. I found myself spending Thanksgiving Day and the following weekend holed up with several colleagues preparing a lengthy presentation to attract more of John Crane's business. Norris and Farmer took the proposal to the president of John Crane, Roger Fix. To my knowledge, nothing ever came of the meeting, and I never knew why.

As time passed, Morgan AM&T went back to the table several times in an effort to develop a business relationship with John Crane that focused on cost reductions benefiting both companies. John Crane's purchasing executives had been directed to cut supplier costs, and we made agreements to drop prices in exchange for volume, but the purchases never materialized. Throughout my career at Pure Carbon Company and Morgan AM&T, I was privileged to work with many hard-working, talented people at John Crane, even though our dealings were sometimes contentious. John Crane was our biggest customer and I always appreciated their business. This course of events was another sign of erosion that was frustrating and disheartening.

During this time, 1998–1999, Waldheger, global president of Morgan AM&T, was promoted to chairman of the Mechanical Carbon Division of Morgan Crucible, and I was named to replace him. (I wasn't Waldheger's first choice for the job, but the performance of Morgan AM&T–The Americas couldn't be ignored.) On the electrical carbon side, Bill Macfarlane, CEO of Morgan Crucible and a close Norris ally, was named chairman of the Electrical Carbon Division. The arrangement was short-lived, though. Waldheger soon moved to research and development, and Macfarlane assumed leadership of the Mechanical Carbon Division, as well.

I believe the move to consolidate the electrical and mechanical businesses under Macfarlane was an effort to keep Waldheger from learning about a grand jury subpoena served on Morgan Crucible in 1999 that alleged the company was involved in cartel activities. The subpoena was a closely guarded secret known only to those involved. I don't believe Waldheger had any knowledge about the subpoena or the cartel—I sure didn't, even though I was smack in the middle of it.

Chapter 3
SAME GAME, NEW RULES

I N MY NEW POSITION AS GLOBAL PRESIDENT, I TRIED AGAIN TO resolve our business opportunities with John Crane in a positive manner and was determined to figure out what was wrong with our European business. At the time, Morgan AM&T–Europe had manufacturing sites in Redditch, Gosport, and Morriston in the United Kingdom, and there were plants in Luxembourg, Italy, and Germany. The Luxembourg plant was a multi-purpose facility that primarily machined carbon-graphite materials for the German market, and it was Morgan Crucible's most profitable European carbon operation.

Because I was traveling so much, management approved of my decision to move my family from St. Marys back to Orlando, Florida. Our oldest daughter had actually stayed there with good friends in order to finish her senior year of high school (stretching her mother's instincts and convictions), and Candy was ready for full-time sunshine. I would be close to Orlando International Airport, so Florida once again became my family's home base while I spent considerable time evaluating and unraveling the mess in Europe. In fact, I left my poor wife and children with unpacked moving boxes stacked in the garage of our new home while I spent weeks at a time overseas, further testimony to Candy's patience and devotion.

I knew Laurence Bryce was a favorite within the Morgan Crucible hierarchy, but my relationship with him deteriorated. He simply wouldn't shake up the status quo and pursue new business opportunities in Europe. I continually offered support and encouragement, but his team's poor performance brought added pressure on Morgan AM&T–The Americas to cover the European profit shortfall. I wrote him, "Laurence, I have never experienced a problem with your management style personally and have always viewed your performance in a positive light. Unfortunately, I have inherited a situation that must be resolved in a positive, professional manner."

I sent a series of memoranda to Bryce beginning in April 1999 that clearly stated my expectations and put him on notice that the buck stopped with him in Europe. In June I sent detailed directions about the incoming order rate, overhead reductions, expenses, and focus accounts. A July memo titled "The Way Forward—Europe" clearly defined objectives and areas where Bryce needed to focus all his time. I concluded by writing, "Politics are non-productive and destructive. It is a cancer in any organization and I am determined that it will be eradicated from any organization I manage. I want performance, not excuses, and a reward system that recognizes excellence, not favoritism, and an organization that speaks its mind objectively and fairly." My managers knew the "Three Capitol P's: Perspective, Position, and Performance." I could only conclude that Bryce's efforts in Europe were poorly organized and his team lacked any direction.

During the period I was communicating with Bryce, I spent considerable time at the Gosport plant in the United Kingdom addressing operational issues, and decided to convene a Focus Accounts meeting there in October 1999. Bryce was scheduled to make a presentation on new business opportunities in Europe at the time. He was first on the agenda—and the last. From the start, his report was obviously a contrived attempt to cover a lack of progress. I abruptly stopped the meeting after barely a minute and walked out. After nearly a year of working with Bryce, I was convinced he had to be replaced.

Any personnel decision like this is difficult, but I had no idea my actions were rippling consternation through Morgan Crucible and the rest of the carbon cartel. Knowing what I do now, Bryce was clearly doing his job—for the network of carbon companies bound by rules of cooperation, not competition! I wanted him to fight for market share, and he was doing the opposite. Our goals were in direct conflict, but I just couldn't figure out why. I thought maybe he had hit his career stride years before and simply lost his competitive edge and become complacent, even lazy.

Heading home to Orlando that afternoon, I tried to call my boss, Bill

Macfarlane, before boarding the plane to let him know I was replacing Bryce, but I couldn't reach him. As soon as I arrived home that evening, Candy told me Macfarlane had called. I returned his call and described the Gosport meeting to him, and tried to encapsulate the months of unsuccessful attempts to get Europe back on track. Macfarlane said that after I left Gosport, Bryce ran up and down the halls bemoaning how much he had sacrificed for Morgan Crucible. Norris stated Bryce was to be reinstated immediately.

"If that's his position, then I resign," I snapped. "Bryce must go. He's killing Morgan AM&T in Europe and dragging down the entire organization."

Macfarlane took my reply back to Norris, who resolved the issue by reassigning Bryce as technical director of the Carbon Division, reporting directly to Macfarlane (who later said my stance made his position with Norris easy). The move by Norris concerned me, but removing Bryce as vice president and general manager of Europe gave me the opportunity to step in and address the problems and opportunities firsthand.

Several months after I assumed responsibility for Morgan AM&T–Europe, Bruce Farmer, Chairman of the Board of Morgan Crucible, called an emergency meeting of the board to hear first-hand reports relative to the issues leading to the overall poor performance of Morgan Crucible. The global presidents, numbering eight at the time, were asked to make presentations to the board that addressed the performance of our respective businesses, including question-and-answer opportunities. My presentation went well, despite ongoing issues in Europe, since Morgan AM&T was still on target to meet the 2000 budget. (Interestingly, Richard Perle did not attend this meeting and resigned from the board shortly thereafter.) My report elicited few questions and comments, and Bruce Farmer called for a recess. He then walked around the room to my side of the table and leaned over, wanting to know, in no uncertain terms, what in heaven's name was going on in Europe.

"If you have a half-hour or so, I'll tell you," I said.

I never heard another word from Farmer. Did he assume I was part of the cartel? Or was he? I wasn't sure, but he previously told Larry Thorwart and me that Morgan Crucible had intervened to stop the sale of Pure Carbon Company to Turner and Newell. What did this all mean?

Quite frankly, the mess I inherited in Europe was shocking. The financials for the four-year period preceding my takeover clearly spoke to a business that was in serious trouble. As I began to analyze the condition in Europe, the sheer depth of the issues I was facing began to surface. What I failed to see, at the time, was that Morgan Crucible was a company heavily embroiled in a cartel, and the cartel activities were ongoing despite my efforts to the contrary. There was no question in my mind I could resolve the operational and sales issues, but I was now playing a much different game—I just didn't know it at the time.

My experience told me there was a wide disparity between prices charged to European customers and those for similar items in the United States. Prices were generally two-to-three times higher in Europe, leading me to question why Europe wasn't profitable. There was no system to track orders, and customer service was abysmal. Morgan AM&T–Europe was on life support, and an infusion of new management was the only way to bring it back. I moved to create an outside board of directors or oversight committee; Dave Quinn and Gene Addesso from the board of Morgan AM&T–The Americas accepted my request to serve in the same capacity in Europe.

Germany was our largest European market for products, but only one salesperson was assigned to the entire territory. I divided the region into four sections, each with a dedicated salesperson as well as application engineering support, a Morgan Crucible core competency that previously was never utilized in Europe.

In late March 2000, Norris's secretary called and said the Morgan Crucible Executive Committee was convening the next day at Gosport and wanted a full presentation on the status of the European carbon business. I was able to put together a two-hour presentation on short notice because I documented our progress in graphs reflecting key performance measurements after I assumed responsibility for European operations. At the Gosport meeting I proposed setting up a manufacturing operation in Hungary, where labor costs were 70 percent below those in the United Kingdom, and reducing overhead and inventories at selected operations. I also suggested moving materials production from the Morriston plant in Wales to Coudersport, Pennsylvania, because Morriston produced only 10 percent of Coudersport's volume but at significantly higher costs.

I emphasized how much progress had been made in a short period of time after nearly five years of declining orders, sales, and profits. Since taking over Europe, financial results showed steady improvement with a significant upturn in March, and the Gosport plant reported its first profit in several years. I forecasted continued growth, better service, lower costs, and improved operating profit going forward.

My optimism compounded my shock a few weeks later when Macfarlane announced that he and Ian Norris decided someone else, namely Julian Bourne, would take over European operations. They wanted me to go home and rest up a while, and Bourne would continue reporting to me.

"You must be kidding! Bourne's a smart guy, but he doesn't know anything about our business. I've busted my butt for six months to turn Europe around, and now, without any input from me, you decide to put him in charge of Europe?"

I obviously ruffled a lot of feathers when I terminated Bryce, but management changes since then were generating positive results, and on top of that, there were candidates more qualified and better prepared for leadership than Bourne. The decision not only disheartened me, but also impacted the new members of the European team; they'd worked day and night for months, and I had assigned my American colleague, Floyd Gerber, to Europe to assist with implementing necessary changes. These people felt betrayed.

The illogical move added to my growing frustration and disillusionment with Morgan Crucible. As an example, Macfarlane had recently insisted I terminate Morgan AM&T's chief financial officer, Everett Chorney, explaining that Morgan Crucible wanted CFOs trained at its headquarters who knew and practiced their accounting standards. The company also cancelled the bonus program that was based on the individual performance of each global business unit and replaced it with one predicated on the overall success of the entire company. (The change only affected two of the eight global presidents because we were the only ones who consistently met or exceeded budget.) It also became clear that while Morgan AM&T personnel spent considerable time developing and executing capital budgets related to strategies for growth, cost reduction, and improved profitability, several other global businesses failed to develop and execute business plans, resulting in shortages that cost Morgan AM&T 90 percent of its approved capital budget in 2000.

Finally, adding salt to my wounds, when I presented the 2001 budget to the Morgan Executive Committee in late 2000, I was informed the administrative costs were incorrect. The Carbon Division controller put a chart on the overhead screen that showed Edye Thein and Laurence Bryce's salaries and expenses still on Morgan AM&T's books. The two no longer worked for me, and while I could accept paying a percentage of Bryce's salary because he was now technical director of the Carbon Division, I was surprised to see he received a pay raise after I removed him as the vice president/general manager of Morgan AM&T–Europe. I was even more shocked to see that Thein's salary for managing a twenty-five million dollar business in Germany exceeded mine by 30 percent. I appreciated that Thein had worked for Morgan Crucible for more than thirty years, but the pay differential compared to our individual responsibilities just didn't make sense (especially since the plant in Germany performed poorly). In time I'd come to understand the special treatment.

All these events combined left me confused, frustrated, and disappointed. The professionally exhilarating ride with Pure Carbon had turned into an international management quagmire. Nothing made sense. Stuck in a rut with my wheels spinning out of control, I contacted Dave Quinn, former president of Pure Industries and Pure Carbon Company, who was now a member of Morgan AM&T's global board of directors. He was my confidante, mentor, and friend. I asked him to negotiate a severance package for me. The time had come to move on.

> "For I know the plans I have for you," declares the LORD, "plans to prosper you and not to harm you, plans to give you hope and a future."
> —JEREMIAH 29:11

Chapter 4
CALM BEFORE THE STORM

DAVE QUINN NEVER TRIED TO TALK ME OUT OF LEAVING Morgan Crucible. In fact, he decided to step down from the board when I left, in part because he was dismayed at how I'd been treated. Bill Macfarlane once asked him why I insisted on leading the turnaround in Europe.

"That's just his style," Quinn told him. "Scott takes on the tough situations himself." He was right. I could have put someone else in the job, but I was confident I could succeed if I found out firsthand what our strengths and weaknesses were. It was no different than addressing the issues at Syntax in Bay City, Michigan, or working the plant floor at Coudersport. My approach was to get into the thick of a problem and resolve it from the inside out.

Candy, on the other hand, wasn't so sure about my decision to retire.

"I know you've been dealt a difficult hand," she said, "but you're not the type to take it easy for very long." She was right, but I couldn't bang my head against a wall any longer. The move to put Bourne in charge of Europe was the final straw.

Quinn worked with Macfarlane on the details of my severance package, which included stepping down as global president at the end of 2000 and then remaining on the payroll for another eighteen months as a consultant and member of the board.

During one of my last trips to Morgan Crucible's headquarters, I walked past the office of Ian Norris, then CEO of Morgan Crucible, and Norris told me to tell Laurence and Tony to take care of their files—they'll know what I mean. Laurence Bryce and Tony Massaro no longer worked for me, and I didn't know if Norris was referring to Tony Massaro or Tony Elvins, so I didn't follow up on his request. Then in July 2001, Norris called me at my home in Florida and asked if I'd spoken with Tony

Massaro lately, who was now global vice president of sales for Morgan AM&T. I said no, but that I expected to see him at the company picnic. Norris then stated, "Tell Tony he is going to appear on the government's radar. You need to pass this message along." I had no idea what Norris was talking about, but I called Massaro later that day or early the next (the Monday before the picnic) to find out.

"Tony, we need to talk. I'm coming up for the company picnic and I'll be in St. Marys by noon on Friday." I arrived at noon on Friday and went directly to Massaro's office. We exchanged pleasantries and then I asked him about the call from Norris, and more specifically if he set prices or did anything illegal I should be aware of. He assured me he had done nothing wrong. I had no reason to distrust Massaro, although he had always been something of a lone ranger, and I accepted his assurance and told him to tell the truth if questioned about anything.

I had racked my brain for any possible situation that might appear suspicious if Morgan AM&T was under investigation for some reason. Norris's phone call threw me for a loop. Something made him give me that message, and the only thing I could think of was an investigation into some sort of illegal activity. I wanted to be completely upfront about anything I had done that could possibly raise red flags or be misinterpreted, so I told Massaro about some dealings I had in 1996 with Jim Floyd, a former Morgan AM&T employee who was let go after the acquisition by Morgan Crucible and later went to work for Schunk.

Once Floyd had been at Schunk a while, he contacted me a few times seeking price levels for three or four parts we sold to BWIP, and once for a part we sold to John Crane–Canada. I explained to Massaro that Floyd was trying to obtain a small piece of business that Morgan AM&T didn't have with BWIP, but they wouldn't test Schunk's materials unless prices were competitive. Regarding John Crane, it had removed one of Morgan AM&T's materials from its approved list because of an unacceptable spring-back condition, making Schunk the only approved source for that part. Floyd was trying to determine if it would be profitable to invest in grinding equipment instead of using a cut shop to machine Schunk's material and then sell the finished product to John Crane. I further explained to Massaro that Floyd contacted me as a friend because things weren't going well for him at Schunk.

To my knowledge, BWIP never approved Schunk's material, and Morgan AM&T introduced two new materials that won back a portion of John Crane's business. Schunk never invested in the machining equipment and continued to sell its material to cut shops.

In January 1996, Morgan AM&T took away Schunk's largest carbon account in the United States, Owens Corning Fiberglass. Floyd called me again, and this time specifically asked me to change the prices we quoted Owens Corning. I refused, and I told Floyd not to contact me again for any reason.

I explained all this to Tony Massaro that day in July 2001 and told him everything would be OK if he just told the truth. I added, "I will not let you be a fall guy for Morgan Crucible."

Those words would haunt me. At the time, I believed sharing the information with Massaro put everything on the table, but I bitterly regretted that conversation when his desperate attempt at self-preservation brought my world crashing down.

When I left Morgan Crucible in December 2000, I was technically still on the company payroll as part of my severance package. Candy and I were already resettled in Florida where two of our children lived and we had many friends. We easily assimilated back into that community with more time for family, friends, church activities, traveling, and relaxing at the beach. My successor at Morgan AM&T, David Cooper, tapped me for help with employee contracts and negotiations, as well as assessing acquisitions.

My son, Rick, was visiting one August afternoon, and he, Candy, and I enjoyed lunch and a pleasant swim. I had gone back into the house to change clothes when I noticed a man at my front door dressed in a business suit. I was surprised since we lived in a gated community. Candy and Rick stayed out by the pool as I answered the door. He was from the FBI and asked to speak privately with me for a few minutes.

"What on earth was this about?" I wondered. Was one of my friends in trouble? Maybe a relative was under investigation, or something was going on in the neighborhood. I showed him to my office, and he then asked me to close the door.

He had come to serve me with a grand jury subpoena, pertaining to a criminal investigation of Morgan Crucible Company PLC and all its subsidiaries, including, but not limited to, Morganite Industries, Morganite North America Inc., and National Electric Carbon Company Inc. The subpoena also included any directors, officials, employees, representatives, or agents of any of these companies. The investigation fell under the jurisdiction of the Philadelphia Office of the Antitrust Division of the United States Department of Justice (DOJ), and it covered the period January 1995 to the present. It also sought any documents related to any communication between myself and any current or former employees of Morgan Crucible. The subpoena went on to list other companies involved in the investigation: SGL, Schunk, LeCarbone Lorraine, Metcar, and asked for any communication regarding the pricing of mechanical carbon products.

I told the agent I had no idea what any of it had to do with me. I was global president of Morgan AM&T. I had nothing to do with Morganite or Morgan Crucible's electrical carbon manufacturing business. He asked if I had had a meeting with one of my competitors—Schunk, of Germany—in Toronto.

"Yes," I replied, "and I had two meetings with them in Germany, and two in the United Kingdom. We were looking into acquiring their mechanical carbon business." The agent indicated this was precisely what the subpoena was about.

I could not absorb the total impact of what was happening, and the agent clearly wasn't in a position to elaborate with much detail. He waited while I contacted Assistant United States Attorney (AUSA) Lucy McClain in Philadelphia to confirm receiving the subpoena. I showed the agent to the door. As he exited our home, he remarked about the beauty of the area in which we lived, and assured me his visit was discreet and in strict confidence. I was impressed with and thankful for his professionalism. I did not expect to see him again, but then I never expected to be going to prison, either.

"Who was that?" my son asked.

"An FBI agent," I said, and proceeded to explain what happened to him and Candy.

"What on earth does all this mean?" Candy asked.

"Dad, this is like having my heart ripped out," Rick said.

I tried to console them, saying the whole mess would be cleared up in a few days. I wasn't just smoothing their feathers—I figured my name was lumped in with everyone else's because I was an executive at Morgan Crucible, but the ordeal really didn't involve me. The electrical and mechanical carbon businesses were completely separate, and the investigation targeted Morganite, not Morgan AM&T. Still, having the FBI show up at my door was alarming—I'd never had any problem with law enforcement in my life!

"Scott, I feel like I've been punched in the stomach," Candy said. "What's going on?"

"Let's not get ahead of ourselves. I'm sure it has nothing to do with me."

While working at Morgan Crucible, I'd been instructed that any legal matters involving the company or me had to be reported to our headquarters in Windsor, United Kingdom. It was late afternoon in Florida, so it was after nine o'clock in the evening in London. I decided to contact my replacement at Morgan AM&T in St. Marys, Pennsylvania, David Cooper. He then contacted Ian Norris, who immediately called and said there was nothing to worry about.

"This has nothing to do with you or your previous business, and our lawyers will handle everything for you," he told me. He said Sutton Keany, an attorney with the New York City law firm Pillsbury Winthrop, would call shortly. Having Sutton represent me calmed my nerves. I had known Sutton since 1995 when Pure Carbon was sold to Morgan Crucible. He and Jerry Peppers, a partner in the firm, worked with me on the acquisition by Morgan. I developed a close working relationship with Jerry and held both of these men in high regard. As promised, Keany called within an hour with basically the same response as Norris. I went to bed that night feeling much calmer, convinced my subpoena was all a big mistake.

My optimism was short-lived. The next morning, Keany called and said

I needed to get my own attorney because the company needed to keep "an arm's length relationship" with me. He had spoken with AUSA McLain just before calling me, and to his surprise, McClain had indicated that the DOJ would object to his presenting me in connection with the subpoena.

"What is going on here?" I asked. "You just told me last night you were representing all Morganite employees in this investigation! Aren't you counsel for Bruce Muller, Mike Cox, and Mel Perkins (all employees of Morgan Crucible's electrical carbon business)?"

"Yes," Keany said, "but after discussing this with McClain, it turns out the DOJ will object to my representing you. It will be best for you if we have an arm's length arrangement."

I was stunned and angry. I was still on Morgan Crucible's payroll, but I had an eerie feeling the company was tossing me overboard, and I had no idea what lurked below the surface. I scrambled in a panic. I needed someone I could trust. I called a close friend who was an attorney in Orlando, Steve Salley. We had known each other for years, and he helped negotiate my settlement when I left Metalized Carbon, so he also knew a lot about the industry. I explained what happened during the previous twenty-four hours, and Salley said he was reasonably sure I wasn't the target of the investigation and would be cleared. He advised me to document every communication related to the case, written or spoken, from that point forward. Salley's assessment restored some of my confidence and helped me put things in perspective: I was part of the investigation, but not the main focus.

I contacted my former secretary, Diane Bressler, who now worked for my successor, David Cooper, and asked her to make copies of several letters that were in my daybooks. Bressler and I had developed a system to track correspondence by month and year for easy access. I also had some files related to the financial performance of Morgan AM&T in Florida, as well as minutes from board of directors meetings I attended. Several days later, Bressler's package arrived, and I put it unopened on my desk. Soon after, Keany called and said they had hired another attorney to represent me, Jerry Bernstein with the law firm Holland and Knight. We were on a three-way conference call when I mentioned the documents from Bressler.

"You can't do that," Keany said. "Those are Morgan Crucible files, not yours."

"Really Sutton?" I asked. "Well, how am I supposed to comply with the subpoena if I can't supply the Justice Department with the documents they want?"

I became very uneasy. They were treating the files as Morgan Crucible property, separate from my concerns. I needed my own legal counsel.

Keany again promised everything would be fine. "We'll help you with the subpoena," he said. "Simply send the package to Jerry and he will handle everything for you."

I called Salley again and he agreed to help me find a good attorney, but told me to get permission from Ian Norris, who gave me the OK and reiterated that Morgan Crucible would cover my legal fees stating I was indemnified for any costs associated with an antitrust investigation. He also talked with Candy and said to call him day or night if we had any concerns.

Candy and I wanted to believe what everyone said—that this was all inconsequential as far as I was concerned—but doubt, fear, and anger often crept in and shook us. Our emotions were on edge. Everything was happening so fast, but we weren't even sure what was happening. It was like being attacked by invisible forces—we'd eventually learn the onslaught was from our own government, with help from former business associates and Morgan Crucible itself.

"I just can't get a handle on this," Candy said. "Every day, I wake up and all of a sudden it hits me that we're in this awful situation, and it just keeps going, snowballing out of control. I know fear is not of God, but I just want this over."

Steve Salley put me in touch with Chan Muller, an attorney in Winter Park, Florida. I recognized Muller's name from the local newspaper because he'd represented several high-profile clients, and his track record was impressive. Frankly, his smile and mannerisms made an impression of a wily country lawyer. Candy and I had our first meeting with him and his associate, Jim Younger, a private investigator, on August 15, 2001. Candy asked to start the meeting with a prayer. I then explained the series of events up to that point, and Muller told me to prepare a timeline of my career in the carbon industry along with a list of witnesses he could contact. I again explained that Sutton Keany, Morgan Crucible's attorney, assured me that because I was technically still employed by Morgan AM&T, the company (a Delaware corporation) would pay all my legal fees. He later confirmed that arrangement with Morgan Crucible. I gave Muller a deposit of $42,500 for his services.

The following day, Bernstein from Holland and Knight called and told me he contacted Assistant U.S. Attorney Richard Rosenberg about my subpoena. Rosenberg said the government had documents tying me to price fixing, but wouldn't be specific. Bernstein asked if I would be given immunity before a grand jury and was told I would not, at which point he said I would plead the fifth and not discuss the case at all. Later, it was reported that Rosenberg told Bernstein they were merely trying to get my attention.

I explained to Bernstein that I had hired my own legal representation, and he expressed concern that we would look silly bringing Muller in, but at that point, it was time to circle my wagons with people I trusted.

Bernstein's office then sent a fax to AUSA McClain on August 16, 2001, advising McClain he was representing me regarding the subpoena. I immediately contacted Sutton Keany's office, but he was not available, so I left a voice message asking him to advise Bernstein that I'd hired my own legal counsel, and Bernstein shouldn't contact McClain again on my behalf. Apparently this message was never communicated because Bernstein continued contacting McClain.

At first, Keany tried to keep Bernstein involved and I was advised Morgan Crucible would pay both his and Muller's fees. Keany called again. "I'm very encouraged the way things are going." That was easy for him to say—he wasn't accused of price fixing.

I updated Muller on the conversation between AUSA Rosenberg and Bernstein, and, concerned about Rosenberg's position, Muller brought in investigator Jim Younger. He was a retired police chief and trained at the FBI academy. The three of us talked for several hours about Rosenberg's claim that he had documents proving I fixed prices, and I was resolute that it couldn't be true. I told them about the conversations with Jim Floyd regarding Schunk, BWIP, and John Crane.

Because of the important role Jim Floyd would play in the outcome of my situation, a little background is required:

Jim Floyd and I go back many years in our careers, and we'd also been personal friends outside of work. I first met him around 1977 when I was vice president of operations of Pure Industries' Tribon Bearing Division based in Cleveland and Floyd was vice president of marketing for Pure Carbon in St. Marys, Pennsylvania. There was some political infighting at that time over Floyd's appointment, but he soon left Pure Carbon to take a management position at Kyocera in San Diego. Dave Quinn, president of Pure Industries and Pure Carbon Company at the time, saw something in Floyd and rehired him sometime in the mid-1980s as a consultant, and eventually brought him back on board as the president of Frenchtown Ceramics, another subsidiary of Pure Industries. By the time I returned to St. Marys as president of Pure Carbon in 1990, Frenchtown Ceramics had been put up for sale and Floyd was back at Pure Carbon managing our Focus Accounts Program for the development of new business.

During my career, I made it a practice to judge results, not personalities. I have no time for pettiness or politics, and I was only interested in Floyd's sales and marketing performance. I was impressed with his organizational skills and enthusiasm. In the early 1990s, we worked hard to make inroads into Europe, especially Germany and Denmark, and Floyd was a major contributor to our success there. But he didn't mesh well with some of Morgan AM&T's senior managers, particularly Tony Massaro and Larry Thorwart.

During discussions leading up to the sale of Pure Carbon to Morgan Crucible in 1994 and 1995, the management teams agreed that certain synergies had to occur to create a viable deal, one of which was to reduce our overhead structure by fifteen to twenty positions. Jim Floyd's position wasn't among the ones I thought should be made redundant, but when the purchase closed, he appeared on the target reduction list of Roy Waldheger, who was my new boss. I reminded Waldheger that Floyd had access to all our primary business information and argued against his termination to no avail. I figured Waldheger heard from some disgruntled managers who didn't get along with Floyd.

I put together a severance package that basically continued Floyd's salary for one year, which Waldheger reluctantly approved. Roughly three months later, Floyd called to say he'd gone to work for a competitor, Schunk. Of course I was concerned at this news because he had in-depth knowledge of our business and pricing, and while Schunk wasn't a serious threat in the United States market, they were entrenched in Europe, where we were trying to grow. At this point, Waldheger even wanted to cancel Floyd's severance agreement, but I successfully argued to honor it because the agreement didn't include a non-compete clause, and it was Waldheger who insisted on letting Floyd go. The entire situation was difficult both professionally and personally; Candy and I were both friends with Floyd and his wife at that time.

In late 1995 Floyd began to call my office in St. Marys. At first, the conversations were of a personal nature, but slowly shifted to "I need your help." He shared that he hadn't made headway at Schunk and was concerned about losing his job. On one occasion, he was seeking pricing levels for three or four parts at BWIP, saying Morgan AM&T had 85 percent of BWIP's business, and he wanted to go after the other 15 percent, but BWIP wouldn't test his materials unless his prices were competitive. I gave him price ranges for three or four parts. About two weeks later he called again and said the information I gave him was different from what BWIP said the prices were.

"Jim, you asked me for pricing levels," I said, "you never asked for the exact price. Obviously you can get that information by simply asking the customer. You don't need my help."

The second request had to do with the price for a part Morgan AM&T once sold to John Crane–Canada. Due to a spring-back materials issue, we had been removed from John Crane's approved materials list. I tried to call Floyd with this information but couldn't reach him, so I faxed it to him from my office in St. Marys.

Obviously I let our friendship color my professional judgment, but I never felt I was doing anything illegal, and the information I gave him never impacted business at Morgan AM&T or resulted in any disadvantage to a customer. To my knowledge, Schunk was never approved by BWIP and never invested in equipment to machine ceramic components in-house.

After the conversation about John Crane, I became uncomfortable with Floyd's calls. They started out friendly, but quickly shifted to requests for pricing. I asked him not to contact me again and said I was severing our relationship. Despite my request, he called again in January 1996 when Morgan AM&T took away Schunk's largest customer, Owens Corning Fiberglass, and asked me to change our prices so Schunk wouldn't lose the business. I refused his request, of course, and Morgan AM&T kept the Owens Corning business from 1997 through 2000. After that exchange, I told my secretary to refuse any more calls from Floyd.

I explained all this to Muller, and it was basically the same information I gave Tony Massaro when I questioned him about any improprieties at Morgan AM&T. I told Muller that only a total idiot would attempt to fix prices with Schunk in the United States. With only about 1 percent of the total mechanical carbon business, Schunk was never a serious threat to Morgan AM&T–The Americas. In fact, I repeatedly told my team never to lose business to Schunk, or other companies, on price. Our cost position and service were the best in the industry and I had no fear of losing business to any competitor.

Another event I discussed in detail with Muller was a meeting I had about acquiring Schunk's mechanical carbon business. Schunk's sales executive, Joseph Klatt, initiated the discussion in December 1996 or early January 1997 when he called me at my office. I invited him to St. Marys, but he stated he had business in Toronto and asked me to meet him there. I contacted Dave Quinn, who was then on Morgan AM&T's Board of Directors, to get his opinion because according to several sources, Schunk's carbon division was bleeding red ink, but Quinn felt I had the ability to turn it around—I had done it for him before. I then called Morgan Crucible's acquisitions and divestures manager, Cris Richard, at Morgan Crucible's headquarters in Windsor, United Kingdom, to update him on Klatt's proposal. I explained all this to Muller.

"I'll discuss the comments about Jim Floyd with an antitrust colleague of mine," Muller said. "In the meantime, let's start talking to some of the people you have on your list of witnesses. Will Tony Massaro testify on your behalf?"

"Sure, I'll call Tony and tell him what's going on," I said.

Muller later advised me that his antitrust colleague said my actions would not be interpreted as price fixing if we went to trial.

Our first hearing with the U.S. Department of Justice and Assistant U.S. Attorney McClain was scheduled for September 11, 2001. One month before, I received a frazzled call from Sutton Keany, Morgan Crucible's legal counsel.

"We're not playing as a team, Scott."

I couldn't believe Keany turned the tables. "You're the one who said we needed an arm's length arrangement," I replied. "Chan Muller is now my only interface with the U.S. government."

Keany continually interrupted me. "You're not listening to me. Carbone Lorraine is the problem and they have nothing on you or Morgan."

"I know I've never had any contact with them. I'm concerned about what Schunk is telling the U.S. government." I repeated AUSA Rosenberg's claim that they had documents saying I was involved in price fixing.

"It's all smoke; they have nothing," Keany said. "They're just trying to rattle your cage."

The conversation then turned to testimony by other Morgan Crucible employees, and Keany said the government reneged on some immunity deals.

"You know Sutton, I find it strange the Canadians offered me immunity, but my own government is threatening me with a felony." (The Canadian government asked me to testify in its investigation of price fixing in the electrical carbon industry, but I was advised against it because my testimony could possibly be used against me in the United States.)

Keany changed direction yet again and complained about Muller's representation. We finished the conversation by agreeing he would call Muller directly to discuss teamwork.

I was increasingly frustrated—and concerned—about how Morgan Crucible was treating me, but I do believe Sutton Keany is an honorable man who received distorted or false information from several people regarding the overall case, including Morgan Crucible's management.

Jim Younger, Muller's investigator, interviewed several people in-depth to prepare for our meeting with the Justice Department, including Keany.

His narrative was lengthy and included helpful and revealing information, some of which is condensed here:

When Morgan Crucible purchased Stackpole Corporation's Pure Carbon Company in 1995, the U.S. government took a hard look at this acquisition.

The first meeting to dissolve joint ventures between Morgan Crucible and Carbone was in Toronto in 1995. Robin Emerson, Michael Cox, and Bruce Muller represented Morgan. *(I later learned from Emerson that this was the first of many meetings to set prices for electrical products.)*

A federal grand jury subpoena dated April 27, 1999, was served on Morganite Industries that was broad and referred to specialty graphite. Assistant U.S. Attorney McClain said she knew there was price fixing and an agreement on sharing customers. She was interested in carbon electrical brushes for traction and transit customers. I wasn't pursued at that time because I was in the mechanical carbon sector, not electrical. *(I never knew about the subpoena until 2001.)*

In June 2000, McClain told Keany that she didn't receive all the documents related to the subpoena. She said Morgan Crucible was in a sea of grief because cooperating witnesses were reporting price fixing by Morgan. She said it involved European executives, not American. Prices were fixed at a series of meetings in Toronto and Mexico City. Ian Norris, then head of Morgan's Carbon Division, insisted it did not happen and told Keany to give McClain everything.

Keany interviewed everyone involved at Morgan except Robin Emerson, whose position had been eliminated. His job had been to keep track of carbon block shipped from the UK. He was bitter and would not be interviewed.

A Canadian investigator believed there were price-fixing agreements between the companies Carbone, Hoffman, Schunk, and Morgan Crucible. This investigator later told Robin Emerson he was being blamed for setting prices. Emerson called Morgan Crucible's human resources manager and asked to be left alone; he was not part of a cover up.

Morgan Crucible was interested in acquiring Schunk and the first confidentiality agreement was in 1996. *(I had no knowledge of this agreement. I did pursue the acquisition of Schunk's mechanical carbon division in 1997, 1998, and 1999, and was told of a confidentiality agreement in 1999, but never received a copy, even though I requested it.)*

Schunk's employees probably told the government that Scott met with them in Toronto in 1997.

In December 1998, I informed Cris Richard, the acquisitions and divestitures manager at Morgan Crucible, that Schunk was ready to sign a confidentiality agreement and exchange financial information. *(I needed information about Schunk's financial condition in order to assess the viability of acquiring Schunk's mechanical carbon division. I made several calls to Richard at Morgan Crucible's headquarters about my request, but never received the confidentiality agreement or any financial information.)*

About ten days prior to August 6, 2001, Keany received a letter from AUSA McClain asking who he represented. He immediately asked if she was issuing a third-party subpoena and wrote a letter stating he represented Morgan Crucible and all its employees, and I was technically still on the payroll. McClain said her information was that I wasn't anymore, and Keany shouldn't represent me because of a conflict. Keany said I told the FBI agent that served me the subpoena that the meeting with Schunk in Toronto probably prompted the investigation into my participation. *(This explains Keany's overnight reversal about representing me; McClain had asked him not to represent me. I question whether this violated my constitutional rights. I was still on Morgan Crucible's payroll as a full-time employee with benefits for nearly a year after I received my subpoena. In fact, Keany said that a Canadian official involved in the investigation with McClain advised her not to say I needed separate representation.)*

Younger also planned to interview Tony Massaro, vice president of sales at Morgan AM&T and my former direct report. Massaro and I worked together for many years, and I had high regard for his technical abilities, but his personality and actions sometimes caused problems with certain managers. Among the staff group, Massaro was famous for writing poison-pen memos or large-lettered notes on correspondence and often used pet names or references that sometimes left people wondering what he meant. I received one such memo in which Massaro made a reference to "friends," and I asked him about it. He said the term *friends* was Edye Thein's code name for a European business that was machining carbon graphite seal rings for Thein, who then sold them to Johnson Corporation's aftermarket in Europe. I advised Massaro to terminate the practice immediately. Shortly thereafter, the president of Johnson Corporation sent me a letter questioning Morgan AM&T's business practices, saying that I personally signed an agreement not to pursue Johnson's aftermarket. I replied in writing that I had never seen or signed such an agreement. I later visited his Three Rivers office in Michigan accompanied by Massaro and Rich Zegar. During the meeting, he produced a document in which Massaro had signed his name in my signature block. Massaro neither requested nor obtained my permission to do this, and his actions were totally unacceptable. Later, according to my attorney, Johnson Corporation's name would surface with the Department of Justice as another company where possible cartel activities had taken place.

After the meeting at Three Rivers, I wrote a follow-up letter advising the Johnson Corporation that Morgan AM&T no longer wanted their business. The letter basically stated that for many years the Pure Carbon Company had been the research and development arm for solving Johnson's application engineering problems. I went on to say that while we appreciated Johnson's business, we felt the company was making an auction out of the carbon seal ring business and we would no longer accept bid packages from Johnson Corporation. I also put Massaro on notice that his actions were reprehensible and an embarrassment to the corporation.

Despite this bump in the road, I felt Massaro was, without a doubt, one of the most talented engineers in our business. During his career, he became the champion at several of our largest accounts, such as John Crane, Procon Products, Johnson Corporation, and A.W. Chesterton. From time to time, Tony would make commitments to these customers that negatively impacted other department managers and caused some consternation. To others, it often appeared that Massaro wasn't a team player, but simply pursued his own agenda.

At one point, Massaro learned I was pursuing the acquisition of a tungsten carbide business in State College, Pennsylvania, and expressed interest in making a career change if Morgan AM&T were successful in acquiring this company. I invited him to accompany me to Federal Carbide on several occasions, and he was on my short list to become the vice president and general manager of this business if the acquisition was finalized. In addition, prior to leaving the presidency of Morgan AM&T on December 30, 2000, I recommended that Massaro be promoted to global vice president of sales. His promotion was one of several I recommended at that time.

The following is Massaro's interview with investigator Jim Younger. I did not participate in Massaro's questioning or suggest what Younger should ask. Following the interview, my attorney of record at the time, Chan Muller, advised me that Massaro's testimony totally supported my position. I was so confident in what he would say about the Toronto meeting that I never bothered to read his statement until after he changed his testimony and was granted immunity from prosecution to testify against me. Massaro's responses in this interview with Younger would change dramatically down the road when he began to deal with the DOJ, much to my misfortune.

Here is what Massaro told investigator Jim Younger:

> Massaro began the interview by stating that Morgan Crucible manufactures no standard product. Every product is a unique part made for a specific customer.
>
> He was told by F. Scott Brown to accompany Brown to Toronto to meet with Schunk because Morgan wanted to purchase Schunk. Massaro didn't think acquiring Schunk was a smart thing to do, but this was an assignment by his boss and he went. He avoids speaking with the competition. He said it was his duty to go to Toronto because his boss [me] told him to do it.
>
> The meeting was at a time in the company's history when Morgan Crucible had acquired Pure Carbon, Carbon Technology (CTI), and National Mechanical Carbon. These were all competitors and then all one company. Pure Carbon had difficulty figuring out what it was as Morgan AM&T.
>
> At the meeting with Schunk at Toronto, Morgan AM&T representatives were Scott Brown, Robin Emerson, and Massaro. Schunk representatives were James Floyd and Joseph Klatt. James Floyd

had worked for Pure Carbon for ten to fifteen years, and Massaro thought he had had worked with him for that long, but didn't like Floyd. Massaro wasn't aware of Klatt's title, but he was the Schunk man from Germany.

Robin Emerson just showed up. Massaro knew Emerson from Morganite's Morriston facility, a Morganite plant in South Wales. Emerson would get involved in acquisition meetings.

The meeting in Toronto was in January 1997. They arrived at the hotel the night before, and may have seen Klatt and Floyd to say hello. The Morgan AM&T people didn't have dinner with the Schunk people.

Massaro said from his memory, the meeting began the next morning about nine o'clock, and everything ended by two o'clock that afternoon, but that was all from memory. He remembers that Scott Brown got angry in the beginning of the meeting and angrier at the end.

There was no discussion of pricing. Morgan owned the American market as a carbon company.

Schunk's attitude was very arrogant. Schunk said that if you don't buy or you don't come up with an alliance, we're going to take the market away from you. They were telling Morgan AM&T that they would come into America and take our business. It was difficult to have a positive discussion and to move forward because of Schunk's arrogant attitude.

Morgan AM&T successfully competed with Schunk in the market. The mechanical carbon business is a small market. We are not ignorant of each other, but we don't have anything to do with our competitors.

Schunk came to the meeting with this arrogant attitude and decided they needed an alliance. An alliance between competitors is something Pure Carbon had done before with a company called Carborundum. Massaro doesn't know how they would have done an alliance with Schunk, but it would have been a legal, open, up-front agreement between the companies and known to the customers. Morgan AM&T also had an alliance with a customer, Global John Crane.

The purpose of an alliance in the mechanical carbon industry between Schunk and Morgan AM&T could be, for example, Schunk had no manufacturing facility in the United States. Morgan AM&T could have manufactured Schunk products. This would give Schunk manufacturing capabilities that it didn't have, and the end result would be positive for both companies and the customers. The companies would still be competitors and would compete on everything else except the particular products they were making together.

There was definitely a discussion about Morgan acquiring Schunk's mechanical carbon business or entering into some sort of an alliance at the Toronto meeting. Massaro doesn't know who initiated this meeting.

John Crane told Morgan AM&T that John Crane was talking to Schunk about an alliance. Customers give competitors prices and disclose what they are paying their suppliers. The customers do this so they can force the companies to lower prices. Massaro also ran into this with a company called Metalized Carbon.

Morgan AM&T was in the final stage of working an alliance with John Crane. John Crane was looking for one supplier to meet their worldwide needs. At the Toronto meeting, John Crane came up in passing.

The discussion about the purchase of Schunk just disappeared and there was a discussion of how an alliance could be structured to work and be reasonable for the companies and the customers.

Massaro believed that Morgan AM&T was not gung-ho about entering into alliances. Scott was operating as old Pure Carbon, very entrepreneurial and always looking for opportunities to expand. Morgan AM&T had a different vision, that's why we didn't know who we were.

As the discussion of the alliance went on, Schunk's hidden agenda became clear. Schunk, as part of an alliance, wanted Morgan to hand Schunk 25 percent of the American business. Scott Brown got angry and made it clear that this was not going to happen. After that, the discussion was just noise.

Robin Emerson was the listener and took notes, tried to calm the high level of excitement. Massaro wondered what Robin Emerson's agenda was when he came to the Toronto meeting. Massaro does not believe he's spoken with Robin Emerson since this meeting. Massaro has been to Morriston, the Morganite plant in South Wales and may have seen Emerson, but does not believe he spoke with him.

Massaro said that if Schunk got any business in the United States, they got it on pricing. In March or April of 1997, Morgan AM&T got the alliance with John Crane (North America), and the contract was based on quantity pricing. Instead of receiving the standard price, Morgan AM&T took into account the total number of parts that Crane agreed to purchase in two years and gave them that quantity discount price. The prices themselves were not dropped or changed, but John Crane received consideration for the quantity they were buying and this resulted in a discount.

Massaro said to the best of his knowledge, Schunk still has some business with John Crane. As far as he knows, Morgan AM&T kept what business they had and Schunk kept what they had. Over the two years of the alliance with John Crane, Morgan AM&T gained market share because of the quality of Morgan AM&T products and the level of service they provided John Crane.

Massaro believed that Morgan's prices were given to Schunk by John Crane prior to the Toronto meeting. Morgan is still the major supplier to John Crane.

If Morgan AM&T had entered into an alliance with Schunk, prices should have gone up. Massaro said there was an alliance (with John Crane) and that prices went down 8 to 12 percent. An illegal price-fixing agreement is to raise prices, not lower them.

Massaro said Scott Brown is under the impression that John Crane actually threw out the 1997 contract. Scott signed a new agreement in early 2000, with the old one still running even though John Crane wasn't living up to its end of the contract.

In the contract Scott Brown signed in January 2000, Morgan AM&T dropped the prices 7 percent in the first year in the United States. Massaro said John Crane didn't do the things they were supposed to do in the contract. In January of 2001, John Crane would receive a further decrease of 3 percent in the United States and Europe. Massaro said he refused to drop the price another 3 percent in the United States and John Crane accepted this. They got the 3 percent decrease in Europe because the European division of John Crane lived up to the contract.

The contract discussions ran from March of 1999, when the old contract should have expired, to January of 2000. Morgan and John Crane continued to work under the old contract until the new contract went into effect.

Massaro said if there was any price collusion, Scott Brown would have to tell him what prices to charge. A review of the current pricing and the historical pricing would show that where there was competition that the cost remained the same or went down. These costs per unit can be obtained from Morgan AM&T's computer system.

In January 1997, John Crane asked for pricing for one thousand parts. Massaro's impression is that John Crane took the price list and gave them to the competition.

Massaro said he doesn't know if Schunk quoted John Crane. Morgan AM&T cut its price 7 percent and kept business because Morgan AM&T had proven grades and proven capabilities. Crane wanted to do business with Morgan because change causes problems.

Morgan AM&T produces one thousand parts that are unique products and grades specifically made to John Crane's specifications. It would be hard to fix prices on one thousand items, which have a pricing history that goes back ten to twelve years. *There was no price fixing* and certainly not at the Toronto meeting. The items are diverse and unique to each part number and customer. To do something like price fixing would require constant communication between the competitors. The communications would be overwhelming.

Prices in the mechanical carbon business are depressed because customers are playing suppliers against each other. You have to be careful of the customer who will tell you that a part you are selling to them for 38 cents, they can get for 31.5 cents from a competitor. You have to ask yourself, is the customer telling you the truth? Can they really get it for 31.5 cents? Morgan AM&T could then choose to meet the price or not. The last quote to John Crane would have the normal quantity pricing breaks.

Massaro became global vice president of sales in November 2000. The vice president of marketing in Europe was John Herke, who worked for Massaro since November 1, 2000. Edye Thein was the general manager of Morgan's Luxembourg operations, Morgan's mechanical carbon operation on the European continent.

Thein sets the prices in Europe for Morgan AM&T–Europe and also for Morgan AM&T–The Americas sales in Europe. Laurence Bryce was vice president and general manager of Europe until Scott let him go.

We lost more than four million dollars, a lot of business in Europe. Morgan AM&T–America did a lot of business and was successful selling a lot of product from the United States in Europe. Massaro believes Bryce and Thein took business away from Morgan AM&T–the Americas and transferred that business to other Morgan Crucible companies in Europe.

We lost business to the competition, but Massaro doesn't know why. Bryce and Thein had direct contact and access to the European customers (of Morgan AM&T–The Americas). Bryce and Thein never provided good data.

The bottom line is that the Morgan AM&T–The Americas business in Europe disappeared. It either went to other Morgan companies or to European competition, but (Massaro) doesn't know why.

Massaro doesn't know what Bryce did with the prices. Bryce had all the right in the world to raise or lower prices. Bryce's job was to increase European business.

The pricing history is there. It would be the market price. It's obtainable by part number and the profit margins would be in the notes. From 1997 to date, the prices have gone down.

The five biggest customers of Morgan are John Crane, Chesterton, Flowserve, Procon Products, and Franklin Electric.

Massaro estimates Pure Carbon mechanical sales in the U.S. to be about forty-five million dollars.

As far as training and antitrust law, Massaro read a letter from Sam Parkhill, who was a lawyer and president of Stackpole Corporation, to all Pure Carbon employees telling them not to talk price to any of the other suppliers or competitors because the practice was wrong and illegal. Anyone caught doing this was wrong and the company would not back them.

Following the Toronto meeting on January 29, 1997, Massaro and I never discussed Schunk again until I questioned him regarding Ian Norris's message about his files and that he was going to appear on the government's radar. It was during this meeting that I explained what occurred with Jim Floyd at Schunk. The only other time Schunk's name came up was at staff meetings or long-range business development meetings where Massaro was a participant, and I'd always tell him, "Don't lose business to Schunk or any other competitor on price." In developing the 1998 long-range business plan, Schunk was identified as the only carbon acquisition target that made any sense. Our management team spent considerable time debating the merits of acquiring Schunk.

Massaro's statement to Younger was mostly accurate as it applied to me, even though he left out critical information regarding his own actions at the Toronto meeting. As we prepared for the hearing with the U.S. Department of Justice, I held fast to faith that the truth would resolve the issue and my nightmare would be over. I found out much later that when Morgan Crucible's law firm, Sullivan and Cromwell, confronted Massaro with a lengthy document he sent to Robin Emerson in Europe following the Toronto meeting, his story changed dramatically—and so did my fate.

Chapter 5

OUT IN THE COLD

SEPTEMBER 11, 2001 WAS A HORRIFIC DAY FOR OUR COUNTRY. I believe all our lives changed forever when terrorists attacked the World Trade Center, the Pentagon, and crashed a plane full of innocent people into a field in Pennsylvania. I awoke that morning full of my own personal dread, which was, of course, overshadowed by these tragic events.

My attorney, Chan Muller, and his investigative partner, Jim Younger, boarded a plane that morning, headed from Orlando to Philadelphia for the first scheduled meeting with the Antitrust Division of the U.S. Justice Department regarding my case. They were only in the air for an hour when their plane was diverted to Charlotte, North Carolina.

I felt the same sadness, anger, and patriotism that most Americans did that day, but I couldn't help the frustration and disillusionment I had about my own government attacking me. I spent my entire adult life up to that point living the American dream—using my education to get a job and advance in my career; working hard and developing loyalty to one company; my family made great personal sacrifices by moving eleven times to support my business success; and Candy and I were very involved in the communities where we lived and raised our children. I coached community and public school sports for years and led a campaign to build a state-of-the-art sports complex in St. Marys. We were proud of what we accomplished and very thankful for all our blessings. After all that, the United States government came knocking on our door and were coming after us. My own government was suddenly my enemy. Taken together, these unimaginable events made September 11, 2001 one of the saddest days of my life.

"You've been a fighter from the beginning," Candy said. "You're a man of true conviction and honesty, and I know you want the truth to prevail.

I just sometimes feel as though we don't even know what we're battling, and the legal end of all this is so foreign to us."

That was certainly true—we were in a whirlwind and not sure what to grab on to, so we clung to each other and to God. We knew He wouldn't let us down, even though the fear and pain were overwhelming at times. I continued attending church as much as possible, singing in the choir, attending Bible study, and helping with outreach projects. My pastor was enormously helpful with his support and counsel. Those activities brought some peace to my otherwise frazzled daily existence trying to piece together my defense.

The terrorist attacks and subsequent fallout pushed my hearing back to October 15. Assistant U.S. Attorneys Lucy McClain and Richard Rosenberg were there with other representatives from the DOJ to meet with Chan Muller and Jim Younger.

McClain said she had documents and sworn testimony that I fixed prices and had done so for a long time in the United States and Europe, and although Morgan Crucible employees were instructed to cleanse their files, some didn't follow that advice. The DOJ had evidence that I took illegal measures to protect Morganite's share of the marketplace, provided guidance to competitors, and attended meetings to make these arrangements and exchange parts lists. She went on to say the DOJ was also investigating me for obstruction of justice, and encouraged Muller to have me give up the party line of denying any wrongdoing and step up to the plate. While there were several parts to the case, the government was treating it as one wide conspiracy, and I would be prosecuted accordingly.

McClain then said something that would gnaw at my gut in the coming months: I was the highest ranking executive of Morgan Crucible that the U.S. government had jurisdiction over. I don't know why she believed this, because the executives at Morganite, one of whom was a U.S. citizen, had authority over the electrical carbon business, not me. The entire investigation started because of corruption within the electrical segment of the industry, which was completely separate from mechanical carbon manufacturing. I wondered who convinced her that I was the government's prize in the U.S. I'm sure part of McClain's conjecture was that as global president of Morgan AM&T, I must have been involved, but it simply wasn't true. The big picture was coming into frightening focus—Morganite executives must have been working on a deal with the government, but I was subpoenaed separately and left to fend for myself. McClain told Muller that if I wanted to take the fall myself, then I was free to so choose. She presented the opportunity for me to take a plea and provide material assistance in exchange for leniency, but wasn't sure I would avoid prison time completely. She went on to explain that with information from me, she could build a strong case to extradite Morganite employees from Great Britain, but if I wasn't interested, she'd make a deal with someone else.

McClain also brought up how and why I left the company, suggesting the move was to protect me from the law. Muller countered that I retired because I was frustrated with Morgan Crucible's policies.

Another accusation focused on faxes from home and calls made with purchased phone cards, supposedly in an effort to cover up communication between cartel members. I never purchased phone cards and never sent a fax from home until I moved to Florida in 1999. I used my office phone and fax to conduct business. I had nothing to hide.

Then McClain got to the heart of the matter: she said there was information from not only Morganite employees, but also competitors, that I attended meetings from 1997 to 1999 where price fixing took place. She handed Muller a list to bring to me.

The ammunition was weak. Of the four meetings McClain had, only one had an accurate date and location, the one in Toronto in January 1997. How could I take these accusations seriously? How could the government even begin to build a case with erroneous facts? While I did have meetings with Joseph Klatt to discuss the acquisition of Schunk's mechanical carbon business, none were productive in the end, and one consisted of merely a handshake and agreement to proceed with a confidentiality agreement following our third meeting at the Frankfurt airport in December 1998. Klatt supposedly kept copious notes of our discussions, which is very interesting since I never saw him write anything. Here's the DOJ's list compared to my meetings with Schunk:

Toronto, Canada—January 29, 1997

(Correct date and location, but I was there at Klatt's invitation to discuss acquiring Schunk.)

Frankfurt, Germany—November 8, 1998

(Wrong location! My second meeting took place near Schunk's headquarters in Giessen, Germany. Joseph Klatt thought we had gotten off to a bad start, to which I replied, "I'm still a buyer." In addition, nearly twenty-one months had passed since the meeting in Toronto and Schunk had zero success going after Morgan AM&T's business in the United States.

At this meeting, Klatt told me that Schunk's management group were meeting the following week to finalize and agree on a plan to sell Schunk's mechanical carbon business and he would call me. I told him that that was what he said the last time and that it took him two years.)

London, England—December 4, 1998

(This meeting wasn't with me! The third time I met Klatt was near the Frankfurt airport, and it was a brief encounter. Klatt shook my hand and asked me to initiate the confidentiality agreement so we could begin exchanging information.)

Giessen, Germany—January 7, 1999

(Again, wrong date and location! My fourth meeting with Schunk was held at Morgan Crucible headquarters in Windsor, United Kingdom in March 1999. Klatt and Schunk's president, Kutzler, attended, and Ian Norris chaired. My involvement was being introduced to Kutzler and joining the group at dinner in the evening, where we discussed the cost associated with closing German plants.)

I had a fifth meeting with Schunk at Morgan Crucible headquarters in July 1999, chaired by Cris Richard, Morgan's Acquisitions and Divestures manager. Schunk proposed to trade their mechanical carbon business for something of equal value from Morgan Crucible, an idea that was unacceptable to Ian Norris, and this was the last time I spoke to Klatt. Interestingly, the DOJ never mentioned the fifth meeting.

If these other meetings took place at these other locations, I wasn't there.

Needless to say, my blood boiled when Muller and Younger briefed me on the hearing. I was unnerved by the notion that McClain said I was the highest-ranking executive in the United States that the government could go after—who convinced them of that? I increasingly feared that the hand reaching over the pond wasn't offering protection, but fingering me as a sacrificial lamb.

Worth noting is the business and political climate in the years leading up to all this. Scandalous corporate greed and crime were unfolding at some of the best-known companies in America: WorldCom, Global Crossing, Adelphia, Enron, and Arthur Anderson. The U.S. government was embarrassed by the magnitude of corruption that left thousands of hard-working people without retirement funds or jobs. The Securities and Exchange Commission (SEC) and DOJ Antitrust Division were in high gear because of the impact of these cases and publicity surrounding them.

In addition, since the mid-1990s the Justice Department pushed to uncover and penalize international cartels using a revitalized Corporate Leniency Program that offers companies and employees immunity from prosecution if they are first to report antitrust violations and cooperate with an investigation. Prosecutors call it the race to the courthouse pitting companies against each other over which will snitch first to protect its people and finances. The strategy is helping uncover international cartels at an unprecedented rate. One aspect of the program is to separate individuals from corporate agreements if they aren't cooperating or are still under investigation, and they are advised to get separate counsel. I guess I was carved (literally and figuratively) from Morgan Crucible's package deal for amnesty. I'm sure federal prosecutors believed I was hiding something and if they squeezed hard enough I'd give them some juice, but I had nothing to offer, and I wasn't going to fabricate a story.

> Reckless words pierce like a sword, but the tongue of the wise brings healing. Truthful lips endure forever, but a lying tongue lasts only a moment.
> —PROVERBS 12:18–19

I actually laughed when I read that McClain said I went along to get along—anyone who knows me at all knows that is not my personality. In fact, I'm sure there are many former co-workers who wished I was more compliant. My attempt to turn around the European market reflected my management style—top management at Morgan Crucible cringed when I fired Laurence Bryce for his lousy performance, but I wanted results, not a gold star, and threatened to quit if Norris re-instated Bryce.

After the October hearing, Younger continued investigating and checking facts, and Morgan Crucible's legal team at Pillsbury Winthrop pored over thousands of internal files. Younger interviewed several more people on the list of witnesses I provided, but Robin Emerson and Jim Floyd, both present at the meeting with Schunk in Toronto, referred him to their legal counsel.

A few months before I was served my subpoena, Jim Floyd called my home in Florida and told Candy he was going to be in Orlando for an American Society of Lubricating Engineering conference. He heard I had retired, and wanted to take Candy and me out to dinner. I hadn't spoken to Floyd in years, but we'd been friends in the past, so I agreed, and also invited him for a round of golf. I found out later that he told the Justice Department it was the worst golf he'd ever seen me play, and suggested I was upset and distracted because Ian Norris had called me in and chewed me out about price-fixing activities in the United States. Norris never chastised me about anything, certainly not for setting prices. I visited Norris's office only once in my entire career to view a presentation for the financial community in London. It was ridiculous that Floyd used that social engagement with me to suggest to the DOJ that I was involved in price fixing. It may seem petty, but I gave Floyd one shot per hole because of his handicap compared to mine, and I lost by only one stroke, so it wasn't such a terrible day on the course for me. I was appalled at Floyd's remarks, but I should have realized anything was possible when people fear for their livelihood and freedom.

Candy and I tried to move forward, longing for the nightmare to end as abruptly as it started, and at one point our hopes lifted. I received a call from Fred Wollman of Morganite Industries in Raleigh, North Carolina, and David Cooper from Morgan AM&T. I was told that there was good news, that the Pillsbury Winthrop law firm had gone through thousands of documents and found no wrongdoing. It was within the discovery stage of my case that I was told I was one of the most honest people they had seen at Morgan Crucible.

I felt relief for a change. Shortly thereafter, David Coker, corporate secretary for Morgan Crucible, contacted me on October 15, 2001, following my attorney's first meeting with the DOJ. He started by telling me the company supported me completely, and then shared a little history lesson. In 1999, a subpoena was served on Morganite with regards to Isostatic Graphite and Specialty Graphite Sales. Carbone Lorraine and SGL Carbon were served at the same time. A year later, the United States Justice Department requested more information from Morgan Crucible. The inquiry centered on Morganite's Railroad Traction business. October 15, 2001 was the day I first learned that Morgan Crucible had been served a subpoena in 1999.

Jack Kroef, Bruce Muller, Mike Cox, and company lawyers met with the Justice Department, which wanted to know about meetings several competitors had in 1995 and 1996. Morgan Crucible acknowledged there had been multiple meetings to dissolve joint ventures.

Near that time, mechanical carbon surfaced as a target of the investigation. Hoffman, a Schunk subsidiary in the electrical brush business, produced evidence that a mechanical carbon cartel was operating in Europe. Morgan Crucible admitted involvement to United States and Canadian authorities.

It (the cartel) started some time around 1936 and was very active in the seventies and eighties in Europe; Schunk was still trying to make it work in the nineties. Schunk attempted to move the European cartel into the United States in 1995 and 1996 through the acquisition of Pure Carbon Company by Morgan Crucible in March 1995. Schunk had their story, but what they said is not what happened, according to Coker.

My jaw was on the floor—a cartel since 1936! I worked for Morgan Crucible for barely six years! Was Coker trying to tell me I was caught up in a sloppy attempt to import illegal antitrust activity to the United States? Assistant U.S. Attorney McClain had said the conspiracy was well controlled. She was right—so much so that I never knew of its existence.

Coker went on to say that Pillsbury Winthrop would no longer represent Morgan Crucible; the company had retained another firm, Sullivan and Cromwell, to handle their legal issues with the U.S. government. Pillsbury Winthrop had thoroughly examined Morgan Crucible's files, represented Morgan Crucible's claims of innocence, and now they were out of the picture. The move was confusing at the time, but later it would make sense to me. I asked Coker if Morgan Crucible was willing to tell U.S. authorities that I had no personal knowledge of the cartel or its workings and he said they would. I began to understand why Bryce and Thein wanted to "review" Morgan AM&T–America's price quotes to European customers.

Attorney Robert Osgood from Sullivan and Cromwell was Morgan Crucible's new lead legal counsel. He proved to be a brilliant tactician, promptly turning over evidence to European authorities investigating the carbon cartel, a move that helped Morgan Crucible escape paying any fines in Europe while other cartel members (Schunk, SGL, Carbone, Conradty, and Hoffman) coughed up total fines exceeding one hundred million dollars! In addition, every American employee working for the electrical side of Morgan Crucible's carbon business involved with price fixing or conspiracy to obstruct justice received immunity from prosecution—including executives that held similar positions to mine, contrary to what AUSA McClain believed about the corporate hierarchy. Osgood also did a masterful job limiting settlement damages in two civil lawsuits filed by electrical customers. All this would come to light down the road for me, but for the time being, my case dragged on. I continued to employ Chan Muller as my attorney, even though Coker periodically encouraged me to fire him.

Shortly before Christmas 2001, Coker called again to tell me Sullivan and Cromwell found no wrongdoing on my part regarding allegations Schunk had made about a customer, Gast Manufacturing.

"I know their claims are fraudulent," I said. "Anyone reading my correspondence files could see that." At least the news added to my sense of relief—for a little while.

Coker then started berating Muller again. They had sent him a joint defense agreement two weeks earlier to which he had not responded. It was actually hand delivered by Sullivan and Cromwell attorney Sam Seymour during a meeting at Sullivan and Cromwell offices in New York on November 4, 2001. They fired their attorneys and suggested I consider firing mine if the lawyers could not come to an equitable arrangement. Coker felt Muller was more interested in chasing fees than representation.

"That's not an option at this time," I said. I was satisfied with Muller's legal representation.

I wasn't convinced of the benefit of a joint defense agreement with Morgan Crucible, but Muller said there was nothing to lose, and we signed it on January 23, 2002. Here are a few key points Muller included:

- I had been assured on numerous occasions by representatives of Morgan Crucible that it was clear I had done nothing wrong, based on a review of documents as well as interviewing knowledgeable witnesses.

- Under the Joint Defense Agreement we would share relevant information, both documentary and the results of witness interviews; our goal was to disabuse the government from any notion that I had committed any criminal conduct.

- We wanted to share the interviews Morgan Crucible had with Edye Thein and other witnesses that support the fact that I was not involved in price fixing or any other criminal act pertaining to the government's investigation.

- There would also be additional relevant documents that supported the fact that I had not been involved in any price fixing.

As part of the agreement, Sullivan and Cromwell's Sam Seymour would come to Florida in February 2002 to interview me. At that meeting, I summarized my work background from 1990 to 2000, and then Seymour asked about my meetings with Schunk.

I explained that I first met Joseph Klatt, Schunk's vice president for sales, in 1992 while visiting the president of Schunk at that time, Dr. Burkhardt Goetze, in Giessen, Germany, to explore whether there was any interest in Schunk acquiring Pure Carbon or forming an alliance to sell each other's materials. The minutes from that meeting with Goetze were well documented and could be found in my correspondence files at the St. Marys office. During lunch, Goetze introduced me to Klatt, and the two of us exchanged business cards. (Later that same year, Goetze visited the Stackpole office in Boston, Massachusetts, and met with me, Lyle Hall, and Sam Parkhill to share ideas and look at various acquisition options. Nothing ever came of the discussions.)

The second time I met Joseph Klatt followed Schunk's termination of Goetze. Klatt called me at my St. Marys office and asked if I would have dinner with Goetze's replacement, Dr. Bruckmann, the next time I was in Germany. I accepted and arranged to meet with Bruckmann on my next business trip, which I recall took place in late 1993 or early 1994.

On the day of the meeting with Bruckmann, Klatt picked me up at my hotel and drove me to a nearby restaurant to meet Bruckmann. Klatt did not join us for dinner, and Bruckmann later dropped me off at my hotel. The meeting with Bruckmann was essentially a rehash of the discussions his predecessor, Goetze, had with Lyle Hall, Sam Parkhill, and me. Bruckmann was also inquisitive regarding Morgan Crucible's acquisition of Carbon Technology in the United States. These two meetings with Joseph Klatt, prior to the Toronto meeting, didn't exceed ten minutes in total, and were hardly the foundation to enter into a price fixing arrangement.

I was asked to meet Klatt a third time in Toronto to specifically discuss Morgan AM&T's possible acquisition of Schunk's mechanical carbon business. My actions prior to and after the Toronto meeting are well documented and are supported by several key witnesses. In addition, my attorney's private investigator, Jim Younger, interviewed Tony Massaro, and Massaro's statements support my testimony in this case. One simply has to read it.

In late 1996 or early 1997, Klatt called me at my St. Marys office about Schunk's mechanical carbon business and we later met in Toronto. Before I went, I discussed the acquisition possibility with Dave Quinn, former president of Pure Carbon, and also contacted Morgan Crucible's manager of Acquisitions and Divestures, Cris Richard. My call to Richard was a mere formality. He didn't want anyone becoming involved in the acquisition of a business without his prior knowledge.

I then told attorney Seymour that when my case unfolded in 2001, I once again contacted Richard, who had left Morgan Crucible. He vaguely recalled my phone call about acquiring Schunk and my requests for a confidentiality letter. Eventually he recalled the confidentiality paperwork to acquire Schunk was initiated by David Coker. How interesting.

I then asked Richard about Robin Emerson and he said he did not know any Robin Emerson.

"Emerson was the employee Morgan Crucible sent to the meeting I attended with Schunk in Toronto, Canada, in January 1997, and I was of the opinion he worked for you as a member of your acquisitions team," I said. He did not recall anyone named Robin Emerson who worked for Morgan Crucible.

I was just plain baffled. How could Richard be unaware that Emerson acted as a corporate representative at an acquisitions meeting? Who was Emerson, who sent him to Toronto, and why wouldn't he talk to investigator Younger about this case?

Finally, when all else failed, I called Ian Norris and asked him, "Who is Robin Emerson and what does he do for Morgan Crucible?" Norris told me Emerson was an employee who worked at the Morristown Plant and represents Morgan Crucible at acquisition meetings to assess inventory levels and discuss plant closures. At the time, Norris's statement made sense, but we later learned what Emerson's real job was.

As my interview with Seymour continued, he asked about a memo I prepared in September 2000 at the request of Ian Norris, CEO of Morgan Crucible at that time. I had just returned to Florida from a business trip in Europe, and Bill Macfarlane called and asked me to fly to London immediately to meet with him and Ian Norris about the organizational structure of Morgan AM&T after I retired. When I met Macfarlane the next morning, he said Norris wanted a report about my meetings with Schunk. There was no explanation and certainly no mention of a subpoena. I figured someone from Schunk complained about my attitude. I summarized the meeting at Giessen, Germany, the Toronto meeting, and the fifth and final meeting at Morgan Crucible's headquarters in July 1999. These were the three encounters in which I was the company representative and the agenda was acquisition.

Macfarlane later claimed the list represented either a summary of companies I'd dealt with since taking over as global president or it was a list of companies I'd met with in connection with the subpoena. Neither statement was true—Macfarlane specifically asked me to compile a list of meetings with Schunk. He didn't explain why, and I didn't find out about the April 1999 subpoena served on Morgan Crucible until after I received my subpoena in August 2001.

Seymour wanted to know if I had a copy of the memo, and if I had marked, "attorney privileged information" on it. I said no to both questions; I had addressed the memo to Norris, and I specifically saw Macfarlane hand it to Norris. At the time I compiled the list for Norris, I had no idea there was any type of investigation going on, but apparently Macfarlane or Norris later served up the memo as an example of my participation working with Schunk to fix prices.

The interview with Seymour lasted several hours. I tried to drum up confidence when he said I was the most credible witness he'd talked to, but I was learning to keep my expectations in check. In all candor, though, I thought the interview with the Sullivan and Cromwell attorneys had gone well. I still had some concerns, especially the amount of time Sam Seymour and his colleagues spent questioning me about the Schunk report Bill Macfarlane had asked me to write for Ian Norris. I left the interview that day feeling Sullivan and Cromwell and the Morgan Crucible board members assigned to oversee and coordinate the internal investigation would make a collaborative effort to determine who had broken the law, if anyone. After all, David Coker, the secretary to the board and a member of the Oversight Committee, had told me that Sullivan and Cromwell had been hired to remove the wrongdoing.

My concerns about the Schunk memo were warranted, however, when months later I read Sutton Keany's comments relative to what Macfarlane had told him about the report. Macfarlane obviously fabricated a story to hide his real intentions, and from his comments I could see I was in the thick of a conspiracy being woven at the highest levels of Morgan Crucible.

As I look back at the record of events that followed, I see a law firm, Sullivan and Cromwell, with a primary interest to limit the collateral damage to its client, Morgan Crucible, with little or no concern for certain individuals, especially me. How else could anyone explain why Sullivan and Cromwell never gave me the opportunity to address the claims made by Massaro after he changed his testimony? I now had Massaro's eight-page statement to Jim Younger that supported my testimony in the case. This wouldn't be the last time Sullivan and Cromwell disappointed me, but their lead attorney Robert Osgood reminded me a time or two that I had never been their client.

So much for rooting out the wrongdoing.

Things got quiet for several months after the Sullivan and Cromwell interview. I talked with Tony Massaro, who still worked for Morgan AM&T, and he said he was grilled by Sullivan and Cromwell's attorneys at their New York offices. I contacted him a few weeks later to see if anything else had transpired—at which point he let me know his attorney had advised him not to discuss the case with me.

What was going on? That was the last time I talked to Massaro. I later learned that Sullivan and Cromwell or the DOJ had documents that Massaro had sent to Robin Emerson in the United Kingdom, which Emerson then forwarded to Edye Thein at Morgan AM&T in Luxembourg. Thein then sent them on to Joseph Klatt at Schunk. Massaro reportedly told the DOJ that I instructed him to send the information—a pricing sheet—to Emerson. This was a total fabrication.

December 4, 2001 was a *smoking gun* day as it related to my criminal case. Robert Osgood, lead counsel for Sullivan and Cromwell, and attorney Sam Seymour who worked out of Sullivan and Cromwell's New York office, met with my attorney at the time, Chan Muller, and private investigator Jim Younger, at Sullivan and Cromwell's New York City office. Investigator Younger provided a detailed report of the discussions that day, including comments by Osgood and Seymour that Sullivan and Cromwell represents all of Morgan Crucible, its subsidiaries, and all its employees. I found this statement perplexing since I had previously been issued a third party subpoena. Despite this fact, Seymour presented a Joint Defense Agreement to my attorney during this meeting. One would have to conclude that Sullivan and Cromwell were representing my best interests also, since they were asking me to enter into a Joint Defense Agreement with Morgan Crucible.

During the meeting Seymour and Osgood stated they had spoken to Schunk's legal counsel, Scott Megregian. The report states Megregian shared information with Osgood and Seymour that Schunk employee James Floyd said the meeting in January 1997 (I assume they are referring to the January 29, 1997 meeting in Toronto) between Floyd and Brown, and after, were meetings to reach agreements on fixing prices and allocating market share in the United States. Also, that in January 1997, F. Scott Brown and James Floyd came to the above understanding, which was followed by three subsequent meetings.

I found the remarks, outlined in Jim Younger's report of December 4, 2001, by Osgood and Seymour most interesting. I believe Jim Floyd either has a poor memory, a convenient memory, or experiences periods of self-imposed amnesia. Here are the facts and some of Osgoods' and Seymours' other comments found in Younger's report as follows:

Seymour states that Sullivan and Cromwell represented all of Morgan Crucible, its subsidiaries and all of its current employees. *(On December 4, 2001 I was a current employee.)*

Osgood and Seymour state they have received information from Floyd that I conspired to set prices and allocate market share with Schunk. *(The statements attributed to Floyd are simply not factual. Following the meeting in Toronto, I never met with or spoke with Floyd again until he called me at my home in Longwood, Florida, on May 22, 2001. Floyd was correct on one point: the Toronto meeting was a price fixing meeting, but the price fixing, the participants, and the details of exactly what occurred all happened after I left the meeting. I have provided the details of what actually occurred to the Department of Justice and those details are now a part of the record.*

The remarks attributed to Floyd are possibly a reference to four meetings I had with his boss, Joseph Klatt, following the Toronto meeting in which Floyd was never a participant. Again, I have documented these four meetings elsewhere in this book. The Department of Justice only refers to three meetings I had with Schunk. Actually, there were five, all for the purpose of acquiring Schunk's mechanical carbon business.)

Osgood and Seymour once again state that in January of 1997, F. Scott Brown and James Floyd came to this understanding and that they had three subsequent meetings. *(After the Toronto meeting, I neither met nor communicated with Floyd in any manner until he visited me and my wife at our home in Longwood, Florida in 2001.)*

The smoking gun—Osgood states there was a meeting in Mexico City, Mexico that was held to implement the understanding to give Schunk a percentage of the business in the United States. *(This statement by Osgood is a smoking-gun revelation. I have never been to Mexico in my life and that is easily verifiable by examining my company travel records, or my passport records. The key questions here are: who were the participants in the meeting in Mexico City, and why wasn't my attorney provided with their names? Remember, it was Sullivan and Cromwell's attorneys who presented my attorney with a Joint Defense Agreement at this meeting. The Joint Defense Agreement was signed and returned to Sullivan and Cromwell on January 23, 2002, despite the fact I was not convinced of the benefit of executing this agreement. When the signed Joint Defense Agreement was sent to Sullivan and Cromwell, it was accompanied by a letter from attorney Muller which stressed several points, one of which was his understanding that Sullivan and Cromwell would share relevant documents that supported the fact that Scott Brown has not been involved in any price fixing. To my knowledge, this never occurred. It is obvious someone knows the identity of those individuals who attended the meeting in Mexico City. I have no knowledge of either the meeting in Mexico City or the individuals who attended this meeting. The question remains, did the Department of Justice know who attended this meeting?)*

Osgood states that Joseph Klatt and James Floyd have been interviewed extensively by the Department of Justice and are cooperating. *(The statements given to the authorities by Klatt and Floyd were false and they deliberately fabricated a story to cover up what actually happened at the Toronto meeting. Also, since Floyd and Klatt were so cooperative, let's hear their explanation relative to a meeting that took place on January 30, 1997, the day after the infamous Toronto meeting on January 29, 1997. Regrettably, the truth about the meeting will never come from Floyd or Klatt, so maybe I should refresh their memories. This was a meeting between Klatt, Floyd, and Robin Emerson wherein*

Klatt and Floyd solicited Emerson's help to get Ian Norris to intervene and have me back off Schunk's business in the United States. Emerson would later tell me he took the matter up with Laurence Bryce, but I never heard from anyone about Klatt's complaint.)

Osgood states that Schunk is enthusiastic in the way it is volunteering information on Morgan. *(I can only speak for Morgan AM&T. I am proud of the way Morgan AM&T and I personally competed against Schunk's mechanical carbon businesses, both in the United States and later in Europe, when I became global president in October 1998.)*

Osgood states that Schunk has its own agenda. *(This was quite obvious to me.)*

Unfortunately, when evidence supporting my innocence or pointing the investigation in a different direction was discovered, it was never thoroughly vetted. I fully cooperated with Sullivan and Cromwell's investigation. I agreed to a lengthy interview with Sam Seymour and two of his associates at Chan Muller's office, and I answered all of their questions fully and honestly. I feel I was entitled to the same representation and protection afforded other Morgan Crucible employees given the responsibility assigned Sullivan and Cromwell by the Morgan Crucible committee overseeing the criminal investigation. I find it somewhat appalling that two different law firms and the United States Justice Department spent twenty-seven months investigating Morganite's electrical business, before the investigation was redirected to me, but no individuals at Morganite or National Electrical Carbon in the United States were ever prosecuted for fixing prices. Most interesting, Morganite, Inc. has paid out millions of dollars to settle customer lawsuits, yet plaintiff's attorneys continue their investigation of wrongdoing in both the United States and Europe.

Then in May 2002, I received several interesting phone calls from Morgan Crucible. First, David Cooper, my successor at Morgan AM&T, said I would remain on the payroll through the end of 2002, instead of July, as was negotiated in my severance package. I heard from Ian Norris about a week later, and my phone system showed the call coming from Bermuda. He asked me to contact him at Morgan's headquarters in the United Kingdom from a secure phone the following day. I telephoned Muller, my attorney, who advised me to take copious notes of the conversation with Norris and refer anything directly related to the case to him. Naturally I assumed Norris thought my home phone was tapped.

I called Norris from my daughter's house, and he once again assured me that I was probably in the clear with the Department of Justice because they were after him and as such, they were pressuring others in order to get to him. I repeated to him that I had zero knowledge of any wrong-doing by anyone in the case or any other matter. He concluded by saying they were after the electrical side of the business, not mechanical.

And there it was again—don't worry... Morgan AM&T didn't manu-facture or sell electrical components... you're in the clear.

Cooper called again in late May informing me Norris wanted me back full time to take over Europe and go after Schunk. "How odd," I thought. I had Schunk in the palm of my hand when I left. I then asked about the organizational structure in Europe and learned the new management team dismantled the quadrant approach I set up for Germany and had gone back to one sales rep for the entire region. I turned down the oppor-tunity, even though Norris wanted me to name my price, according to Cooper. I wondered whether, in the midst of all the legal chaos, he was determined to at least get even with Schunk in the business world.

Chapter 6
ROUND TWO

THE SECOND MEETING BETWEEN MY ATTORNEY AND THE DOJ was in August 2002, one year after my subpoena. Assistant U.S. Attorneys Lucy McClain and Richard Rosenberg began by stating the government believed I was involved in a conspiracy to commit antitrust violations. My attorney, Muller, countered that after a year of interviews, investigation, and access to information through Morgan Crucible lawyers, there was no evidence of price fixing on my part. The hearing continued with the following summarized points:

- The DOJ claimed other documents, not from Morgan Crucible, implicated me, but they couldn't show them to us at that point.

- Muller pointed out that when I took over the European market, I operated with the same vigor I had at Pure Carbon, pursuing customers with attentive service and competitive pricing. The cartel must have told Morgan Crucible to get rid of me.

- AUSA Rosenberg said there was three years worth of price exchanges and witnesses to the conspiracy to keep prices from falling. Schunk was a new competitor in the United States and having an impact. (*Obviously the government had little knowledge of the carbon manufacturing marketplace in the United States. Schunk was not a new competitor and was never a threat to Pure Carbon or Morgan AM&T.*)

- Rosenberg said he hoped I wasn't focusing on the acquisitions meetings because those weren't the government's main concern. McClain added that a case was viable without the documents, too.

- Rosenberg said I discussed prices and customers with competitors, and there were complaints about undercutting each other. *(In discussions with Klatt, the subject of customers surfaced twice. In Toronto, I said we needed to find a way to counteract moves by John Crane to play us against each other. The second was a quote for Procon parts. When I offered the quote to Klatt at the Frankfurt airport, he declined, saying he didn't need it anymore. Selling parts to a competitor is standard practice in the mechanical carbon industry, and usually happens when a competitor finds an aftermarket application for a part they don't manufacture.)*

- Rosenberg said they now knew I wasn't the one who used phone cards or sent questionable faxes. *(No kidding—then who did?)*

- McClain questioned my dismissal from Morgan AM&T, and pointed out I was kept on as a consultant. *(I wasn't dismissed—I retired. My role as a consultant was part of my severance package. Initially, my successor, David Cooper, used me extensively to negotiate employee contracts and evaluate possible acquisitions.)*

- Rosenberg said there were calls to Schunk in 1995 regarding what their prices were. *(I never made these calls or told anyone else to.)*

- Rosenberg said the illegal activity started at the top. I was directed to discuss prices, maintain prices in the United States, and keep Schunk out. *(Management never directed me to do anything regarding prices in the United States. If this did happen, who participated? Schunk couldn't compete against our cost position and has since closed their U.S. plant.)*

- Rosenberg asserted Morgan AM&T was the largest company and could set prices, and then gave them to Schunk so they wouldn't undercut. *(The financial performance of Pure Carbon and Morgan AM&T from 1990 to 2000 shows margins and profits increased each year while prices remained relatively flat. We were the market leader because we had a 30 percent cost advantage over Schunk. I never participated in the crazy scheme Rosenberg described, but I think I know the players who did.)*

- As proof, the government had a fax from me from a Morgan Crucible machine that listed prices higher than Morgan AM&T's quote to a competitor. The list appears to be for John Crane. *(The only fax I had anything to do with was the one I openly sent to Jim Floyd so he could decide whether it was profitable to machine a part that Morgan AM&T no longer sold. I was trying to help a friend save his job. I never tried to hide or camouflage this fax. It was done in the light of day.)*

- Muller suggested I would be a great witness for the government.

- McClain said even though I instructed people to destroy documents and not take notes, we should assume witnesses took notes and kept documents anyway, and assume the government has those documents. Obstruction of justice charges will tilt a jury in favor of conviction. *(I never instructed anyone to destroy documents in this case. The documents destroyed by Massaro would, in my opinion, have been incriminating for him and the person or persons he exchanged information with. Also, I never instructed anyone not to take notes in any meetings I attended.)*

- McClain said I would have to plead to a felony, and she wouldn't use me as a witness without a plea. Bryce and Thein will take advantage of testifying without being charged, but no one higher than me would be a witness without being charged. *(This is somewhat amazing. I can only assume the conspiracy had a life of its own. Bryce and Thein testifying against me in federal court was outrageous.)*

The meeting was an exercise in futility and frustration from my point of view. McClain and Rosenberg also said years of my company travel records were missing. I handled my expense accounts and paperwork according to company policy, and whatever happened to the documentation after that, I don't know. I suggested they should go through my records with the company travel agency in St. Marys, because I was being accused of being a lot of places I never visited.

As far as Morgan AM&T's profits, we were successful because we were good at business, not because we snuck around in the dark passing price lists to our competitors. It simply sounded ludicrous. We solidly kept our market share by cutting costs, providing outstanding customer service, staying ahead of the game with research and specially designed products, and keeping prices competitive. Before Morgan Crucible bought Pure Carbon, we were the world leader in the development, manufacturing, and sales of carbon materials and components, and we had the only Materials Application Bank in the industry that allowed us to quickly identify and recommend material solutions to solve our customers' problems. Every company had to enter the market with lower prices on some parts in order to get them tested and approved by a customer, but it was standard business practice. Nobody from the United States government asked the obvious question: why on earth would I put my entire reputation at risk by participating in this scheme—I didn't need to!

My rebuttals seemed to fall on deaf ears. My wife, Candy, knows I have never been very patient, but she reminded me that no matter what happened, we had to wait upon the Lord and trust His timing, and that's what I tried to do. I became more prayerful and found great comfort in Psalm 25:1–5:

> To you, O LORD, I lift up my soul; in you I trust, O my God. Do not let me be put to shame, nor let my enemies triumph over me. No one whose hope is in you will ever be put to shame, but they will be put to shame who are treacherous without excuse. Show me your ways, O LORD, teach me your paths; guide me in your truth and teach me, for you are God my Savior, and my hope is in you all day long.

Bible passages like this one helped me cope with the frustration and fear that gripped me at times. I often stopped by our church sanctuary just to pray and light a candle, which brought some reprieve. I belonged to the church choir, and for the few hours we practiced and then sang on Sunday morning, I was lifted above my trial. Everyone in the choir knew what I was going through, but they made sure we laughed and rejoiced in the Lord. The minute I walked to my car, though, the burden hit me again, but at least for a while I had peace.

The rector of our church, Reverend Charles Holt, met with Candy and me several times throughout the ordeal and was immeasurably helpful. There was plenty of emotion in those sessions.

"I can't tell you what to do, Scott," Rev. Holt said, "but whatever you decide, I'm behind you 100 percent and so is this entire parish." In addition, Candy and I had friends who were solidly grounded in faith and offered counsel, encouragement, and many prayers. Some people thought I must have been mad at God at times, but I never was—in fact, God was my Shelter and it was only under His wing that I knew I was safe. I really do wonder how people get through life's serious challenges without God!

Pressure mounted to change my legal representation. It was obvious to my family and me that no matter what I said or produced as evidence, no one was buying my story. I finally concluded that I needed an antitrust attorney, and Muller helped me find Joe Tate, a law partner in the

Philadelphia firm Dechert Law. Tate had an extensive antitrust background, an excellent track record, and started his career at the Justice Department after graduating from Villanova University Law School.

Bill Macfarlane called the day before I traveled to Philadelphia to meet Tate for the first time on October 8, 2002, because he and Norris had "good news." The morning of October 9, 2002, Norris and Macfarlane called me at six o'clock on my cell phone as I was boarding a flight to Philadelphia to meet with attorney Tate. Norris said he had retained a Washington DC lawyer, Larry Byrnes, to represent him in the case with the Justice Department. Norris said negotiations with the DOJ had gone well, and Byrnes would soon contact Tate. He added that Sullivan and Cromwell found no mechanical carbon price fixing in the United States. Norris then disclosed that he was stepping down as CEO of Morgan Crucible because he had cancer.

"Carbone and Schunk have conspired to nail me, Scott. You need to vigorously pursue the DOJ," he said.

"Don't worry about me. Turn your attention to your health and get well quickly. I'll be praying for you." These were the last words I have ever spoken to Norris. Following the resignation of Ian Norris on May 8, 2002, Bruce Farmer, the chairman of the board of Morgan Crucible, announced Norris had retired due to ill health. He added that Norris had been battling cancer for two years. Farmer thanked Norris for his enormous contributions.

Later that same day, a second notice was sent out announcing an executive restructuring at Morgan Crucible. Nigel Howard was named acting chief executive. In the same announcement, Bill Macfarlane was named executive director of Morgan Crucible and a member of the board of directors.

Howard's tenure as the acting CEO of Morgan Crucible lasted several months while the board of directors searched for a permanent replacement for Norris. In October of 2002, the board announced that Warren P. Knowlton, an American citizen with extensive management experience, would be the new CEO of Morgan Crucible. Knowlton had a reputation for revitalizing and turning businesses around. He guided Morgan Crucible through a difficult period and was responsible for significant improvements in shareholder stock values, before resigning in 2006. Under Knowlton, Nigel Howard became the deputy chief executive, a position he held until he retired in December 2003. Macfarlane's new responsibilities, however, ended shortly after they started, when he resigned on April 17, 2003. These departures were accompanied with large severance packages in addition to normal retirement benefits, recognized by Americans as "golden parachutes."

Knowlton's appointment ushered in a new era at Morgan Crucible that saw several people accept severance packages and leave the corporation. Some of those who left, in my opinion, were tainted by the price fixing scandals and were asked to leave, while others left of their own volition. In any case, the era of the "new" Morgan Crucible had begun and Knowlton implemented many positive changes.

Mark Robertshaw, who joined Morgan Crucible on October 20, 2004, as Chief Financial Officer, was appointed by the board of directors to succeed Knowlton on August 4, 2006. Under Robertshaw, Morgan Crucible has emerged as a stronger company as a result of several divestitures and acquisitions aimed at supporting the company's core businesses. He has provided much needed capital to support the growth opportunities at several of the larger business units. Robertshaw has the reputation for developing high growth and high margin businesses. The new Morgan Crucible seems well positioned for future growth in the years ahead.

During the meeting to transfer information from Chan Muller to Joseph Tate, I mentioned the call from Norris. Tate was worried, "It sounds like a deal is done or in the works." We soon learned from Sam Seymour at Sullivan and Cromwell that it was true—Morgan Crucible had cooperated with investigators and entered into a plea agreement, but the negotiations didn't protect me, Tony Massaro, Robin Emerson, or Ian Norris. Someone was going to prison—I just couldn't fathom how that person could be me. We would later learn Massaro was granted immunity from prosecution and would testify against me.

Upon hiring Tate, the subject of indemnification had to be addressed again, and he prepared a letter confirming Morgan Crucible Company, PLC, agreed to pay my legal fees, and it was confirmed in that agreement. We received a revision back from Seymour with the changes, "…your former employer has agreed to pay your reasonable legal fees for so long as you continue to cooperate in a reasonable manner with Morgan Crucible in its internal investigation and its dealings." Seymour had also struck his name and added David Coker's, Morgan Crucible's corporate secretary, who previously assured me the company totally supported me. Seymour then told Tate that Morgan Crucible would only cover my legal fees through a reasonable period and would not pay if I went to trial. It was clear that Morgan Crucible didn't want the negative publicity a trial would bring, and I still wonder if the U.S. government pressured Morgan Crucible to cancel my indemnification so I would take a plea, a tactic many business executives and defense attorneys believe is on the increase. On top of all this, Seymour said his firm wouldn't continue the joint defense agreement. I cooperated and was interviewed extensively, but Morgan Crucible wasn't going to reciprocate. This news followed Seymour's changes to Tate's letter, which stated that Morgan Crucible would only pay my legal fees through a reasonable period and would not pay my legal fees if I chose to go to trial. Tate's email to me, summarizing his conversation with Seymour, indicated Seymour was very uncomfortable with the new position taken by Morgan Crucible.

During my next meeting with Tate, he received an intriguing phone call from Schunk's legal counsel Scott Megregian. Megregian stated Morgan Crucible had copped their plea agreement and fine by giving up Scott Brown to the Department of Justice. Tate asked Megregian to disclose the information given to the DOJ in my case, and Megregian agreed to discuss the documents, but added he could not provide anything in writing. He said Schunk was worried my testimony in a trial could cost them millions of dollars in civil lawsuits. He told us a deal could be struck with the DOJ because they wanted Norris, not me.

Well, I didn't have anything to offer about Norris or anyone else, and I wasn't going to invent a story. Furthermore, I told Tate I didn't care if Schunk got stuck doling out hundreds of millions. They deserved to pay. The network of bargaining and legal shenanigans was insane.

Joe Tate is a distinguished, highly intelligent advocate. In all fairness, he took on a case that the Department of Justice had undoubtedly already decided, supported by Morgan Crucible's cooperation and its objective to protect Morganite's electrical personnel. By the time he came on the scene, I was, quite frankly, just plain worn out. For two-and-a-half years I seldom slept more than two hours a night. Exhausted at bedtime, I slept only briefly until a barrage of questions and accusations filled my head. I kept trying to convince myself that justice would prevail. After all, this was the United States of America, and I was innocent. Everything would work out. There were those times, though, when I wished to God that I just wouldn't wake up in the morning. That's when I turned to the Lord and leaned on my wife, family, friends, and colleagues who never wavered in their support and encouragement to fight on.

I'm sure my extreme level of frustration and burden played into my relationship with Tate. In addition, he was relaying a litany of false accusations against me from Joseph Klatt, Tony Massaro, and Jim Floyd, and I was enraged at the game those three were playing. With so much at stake, and so great a need for Tate to rally on my side, our exchanges grew confrontational. He raised questions about my participation in price fixing or obstruction of justice, and I vehemently denied any wrongdoing. In retrospect, he was doing his job, probing and preparing me for what the DOJ would use against me, but when he asked the same question six different ways, I pounded the table and yelled, "My answer is not going to change no matter how many times you ask!" I finally asked Dave Quinn to sit in on our meetings, and at one point, Joe even suggested to Quinn privately that I might be in denial, but Quinn had known me too long. "He's telling you the truth," Dave told him.

In February 2003, Assistant U.S. Attorney Rosenberg began sharing information with Tate and his associate, Christine Levine, from statements Joseph Klatt and Jim Floyd made as part of the DOJ investigation. They weren't allowed to copy the transcripts, but made notes based on their collective memory. The information included testimony about four meetings and a pricing spreadsheet produced by either Morgan Crucible or Tony Massaro. Nowhere is it indicated that an acquisition was the topic at any of the meetings.

Notes related to the Toronto meeting were mostly about John Crane and how each company would protect each other on certain products. There was a list of parts and dollar values (totaling $1.6 million) for business that Schunk wanted. No agreement was reached because Morgan Crucible wanted a 50–50 split. Here are some key items Tate and Levine shared with me:

- Notes from one meeting indicated that Schunk and Morgan would only meet outside the United States, with "RE" (presumably Robin Emerson) as a go-between. There was a reference to distrust, and E. Thein as the source, and it was agreed that all further pricing would be done by "FSB" (presumably F. Scott Brown) and Klatt.

- Notes from either a second or third meeting stated Schunk had improperly taken sales from five customers: Procon, Gast, Franklin Electric, Chicago Allis, and Chesterton. FSB complained about this and said it cost him one million dollars in reduced prices to retain the business. At one meeting, FSB also complained that Schunk had taken business illegally at Johnson.

- The final meeting notes listed what appeared to be a number of John Crane locations and the percentage of business of each that would go to Schunk or Morgan Crucible. One of the notes made a reference to persuading the manufacturer Metcar and others to go along.

- An eighteen-page fax that has a cover sheet from Massaro to Emerson dated Feb. 9, 1997, (after the Toronto meeting) with a spreadsheet of prices to John Crane for hundreds of products. Massaro claimed he prepared the list for the Toronto meeting at Scott Brown's request, but it was not complete, and Schunk didn't have its prices to Crane, (in other words, Schunk had not quoted Crane). Brown told Massaro to take it back and finish it, and send it to Emerson who would then send it to Klatt at Schunk. Massaro followed through and kept this copy.

- There was another Morgan price list, and notes alluding to difficulty as result of European pricing differential.

Rosenberg repeatedly said that nobody corroborated my position that the meetings were about an acquisition. Rosenberg claimed Klatt said John Crane's decision to go to a global contract was the trigger for the Toronto meeting, and Massaro will testify that Morgan Crucible and Schunk needed to come together about pricing. After the Toronto meeting, I supposedly instructed Massaro to prepare a price list of the John Crane parts and send it to Robin Emerson at Morgan Crucible in the United Kingdom, who would then send it to Klatt at Schunk.

Most of this information was false as far as my involvement, and a lot was missing. I can only assume that my responses to the email from Tate and Levine regarding what happened in the Toronto meeting was conveyed to Rosenberg. Massaro's statements were his words and recollections, and not mine. They totally verified my statements regarding the Toronto meeting. Clearly the government was selective in what it researched. The most intriguing and important information had to do with what happened after I left the meeting—but that would not surface until it was too late for me.

Chapter 7
ARROWS IN THE DARK

W HEN MY ATTORNEY JOE TATE HIT ME WITH THE CONVO-
luted information from the notes they had read, I was eager to
respond. As far as the suggestion that I complained about Schunk taking
business at five of Morgan AM&T's customers, an examination of files
and contracts would have proven this simply wasn't true. For example,
we had lost nearly all our Chicago Allis business to another company,
St. Marys Carbon, on pricing. Why would I even have a discussion with
Klatt about that account? We invested several million dollars developing
a manufacturing cell to machine parts for Procon and retained that
account by innovatively cutting costs and increasing profits. All these
measures were documented—I couldn't understand why the DOJ ignored
facts and listened to Klatt and Floyd instead.

Klatt's claims that a pricing battle erupted as a result of a 1997 deal
between Morganite Special Carbon Limited (MSCL) and Flexibox were
also far-fetched. Laurence Bryce was in charge of Europe in 1997 and
negotiated the Flexibox contract, one of the worst I've ever seen; certainly
not something that produced some sort of windfall for MSCL. When I
took over the European marketplace in 1999, the account was a financial
disaster. We consolidated Flexibox's production into one facility in Luxembourg, cutting costs significantly and increasing profitability. I recognized
Klatt's verbiage as sounding like cartel lingo, as did his notes about Morgan
and Schunk compensating each other and manipulating accounts for
one another, but these were conversations with Bryce or Thein (the sales
manager in Europe), because he never had them with me.

Clearly my pivotal problem was the meeting in Toronto. I realized my
freedom depended on recalling what happened nearly five years prior
in a meeting that only lasted about sixty minutes for me, but continued
with Massaro, Klatt, Floyd, and Emerson for roughly one hour more

after I departed. I didn't learn the details of what these four discussed until Emerson and I became inmates at Eglin Federal Prison.

First of all, when Joseph Klatt called me in late December 1996 or January 1997 to find out if Morgan Crucible had any interest in acquiring Schunk's mechanical carbon division, the idea to meet in Toronto was his, not mine. Prior to that telephone call, I hadn't talked to Klatt since sometime in late 1993 or early 1994. I asked Tony Massaro to attend the Toronto meeting to address any technical questions that might arise.

I made the arrangements for the meeting room and amenities at a Toronto hotel. Klatt and Floyd from Schunk arrived about 9:30 a.m., and Robin Emerson, representing Morgan Crucible, joined us shortly after. I had never met or spoken to Emerson before the Toronto meeting.

Before we sat down for breakfast, Klatt engaged me in small talk about Schunk's various businesses. He mentioned several changes had occurred in Schunk's organizational structure since the last time we'd spoken, and he said Schunk had expanded into several businesses they did not understand. Eventually the conversation came around to Schunk's mechanical carbon business, and he advised me its sale was fraught with regulatory issues, and talked about the high cost of closing plants in Germany. I then suggested other possibilities such as a strategic alliance or a joint venture. This conversation lasted about twenty minutes.

The seating arrangement for breakfast didn't seem important at the time, but my future depended on details. It was a big room, and I sat about twelve feet from Klatt, Emerson was off by himself, and Floyd and Massaro sat in close proximity to one another, which should have been a red flag since they disliked one another.

I brought up the issue of consolidation of the seal market by John Crane and Flowserve and the need to find a way for Morgan and Schunk to work together going forward. I also referred to some tactics being used by John Crane trying to play our companies against each other. Those references were the only times I mentioned John Crane that day. What I didn't say was that I'd been working on ways to win Crane's North American contract, including upgrading Morgan AM&T's manufacturing processes. Nor did I say anything about improving delivery performance, submitting lower pricing in exchange for increased sales volume, and investing nearly 1.5 million dollars to expand pressing and baking capacity at Carbon Technology to address potential new business being discussed with John Crane.

Jim Floyd then raised the issue of purchasing disposable phone cards for future contacts, which I questioned. Why would we need disposable phone cards? All my business dealings were on my telephone or fax at my offices in St. Marys. At that point, I reminded Floyd he was never to call me again, although I spared him the embarrassment of mentioning in front of his boss, Klatt, that I'd told him this months before when he pestered me for pricing levels and asked me to raise prices at Owens Corning Fiberglass, which I refused to do.

To my surprise, the first words from Klatt's mouth once we sat down at the conference table was a demand for 50 percent of the resin bonded business at John Crane in the United States. I told him he would have to earn it. Klatt then threatened to buy an American company and try to make things tough for Morgan AM&T. He mentioned Metalized Carbon, and I laughed, "You couldn't buy Metalized Carbon in a month of Sundays."

Klatt became irritated and continued by saying Morgan AM&T had 30 percent of the mechanical carbon business in Europe, and Schunk wanted 30 percent in the United States. I slammed the table and looked him in square in the eye, "You will earn *every penny of business* you ever get in the United States!" That's what I said, that's what I meant, and most importantly, that's what I made Schunk do. After the meeting, I continued vigorously pursuing Schunk's carbon business at every opportunity. My record is consistent; I never deviated for one moment from a mission to either buy Schunk or sink Schunk. Schunk would later close their U.S. plant.

At that point, the meeting turned into a shouting match. Massaro and Floyd were pointing fingers at each other and talking loudly, but I couldn't make out what they were saying. For nearly twenty minutes I just sat and observed the chaos. Realizing I'd been duped into attending the meeting under false pretenses, I was in a slow burn. At about 10:30, I announced I was going to my room to pack, and told Massaro to meet me at the front desk.

At checkout, the attendant told me they had to first inventory the meeting room in order to prepare my final bill. I proceeded to locate

Massaro, but he wasn't in his hotel room, so I returned to the conference room looking for him. When I opened the door, which was nearly an hour after I left the meeting, Massaro, Floyd, Klatt, and Emerson were still together having a quiet conversation.

"We're checking out, Tony, let's go." The other three men moved toward the door where I was standing. I looked at Klatt and said, "If you're interested in selling the technical ceramics or mechanical carbon businesses, give me a call." Klatt shot back that his technical ceramics business would never be for sale, but that he would call me in a week or so about the mechanical carbon side. Nearly two years passed before I heard from him again.

Klatt said we discussed companies protecting each other. I told Tate none of that was true, at least not while I was in the room—I don't know what they discussed during the hour or so I was gone. I reminded him of Massaro's initial interview with my investigator, Jim Younger, when Massaro said he went with me to Toronto to discuss an acquisition and was taken aback by Schunk's arrogance and hidden agenda. Massaro also told Younger there was no discussion of pricing, but Tate figured Massaro would just say he lied during his first "unofficial" interview.

Regarding the revealed notes about another meeting near Giessen, Germany (Schunk's headquarters), Klatt's statements were false and misleading, especially his comment that, "all further pricing would be done by FSB."[1] I couldn't have priced any part without assistance from several other key managers at Morgan AM&T locations around the globe. Thorough investigations by Morgan Crucible's law firms never found evidence that I was involved in fixing prices or pressured anyone to set a price for a customer. Klatt alleged I was upset because Schunk took business from Morgan AM&T, which was ridiculous. Schunk never really was a player, and I certainly didn't feel threatened by them.

Once again, the price list reared its ugly head. Massaro told the DOJ that I directed him to prepare a spreadsheet for the Toronto meeting that included products sold to John Crane, estimated quantity to be ordered, and Morgan AM&T's prices for various quantities. Massaro stated he didn't have time to finish it for the Toronto gathering, so, supposedly, I told him to finish it afterward, and send it to Robin Emerson at Morgan Crucible who would then forward it to Klatt. Massaro told investigator

Jim Younger and I that he thought John Crane took the price list and gave it to the competition. I never participated in this scenario, or any other that shared our prices for John Crane with Schunk.

My five meetings with Schunk including Toronto are well documented. I was the senior manager at the first three, Ian Norris chaired meeting number four at Morgan Crucible's headquarters in Windsor, United Kingdom, and Cris Richard chaired the fifth and final meeting with Schunk at Morgan headquarters in Windsor, which followed the signing of a confidentiality agreement that Klatt and I had agreed to initiate in December 1998. I had contacted Cris Richard to prepare the agreement. After a number of calls to Richard, he informed me that David Coker, Morgan Crucible's corporate secretary, initiated the paperwork. I later found out that the agreement wasn't drafted until April 1999, after the fourth meeting with Schunk at Morgan Crucible's headquarters, chaired by Norris in March 1999. How interesting.

On June 22, 1999, I received a telephone call from Laurence Bryce. Ian Norris had asked him about the status of the Schunk mechanical carbon acquisition. Following the call, I sent the following fax to Norris at Morgan Crucible's headquarters in Windsor, United Kingdom:

Mr. Chairman:

I received a telephone call from Laurence Bryce this morning informing me that you had inquired about the status of the acquisition discussions with Schunk.

Since Schunk's last contact with us in January 1999, only two significant things have occurred as follows:

David Coker initiated and received signed confidentiality agreements related to the possible sale of Schunk's global mechanical carbon business.

We met on March 2, 1999, at Windsor with Schunk's key management to start the acquisition process.

To date, other than the confidentiality agreement, no documentation, financial or otherwise, has been exchanged. Most recently, I was contacted about setting up a second meeting to discuss plant rationalization if the deal was made. I can only assume that the Germans have questions related to what facilities we would utilize in

Germany, if any, since we also have acquired Rekofa in the interim.

I spoke with Joe Klatt via telephone on Monday, June 21, and we have agreed to a second meeting at Windsor on 19 July 1999. The Schunk management would arrive on Sunday evening and we would meet them for dinner. Joe is to let me know who will be coming from Schunk and as soon as I have this information, I will forward it to your attention.

I would anticipate the meeting on July 19 taking most of the day since both Morgan and Schunk have numerous plant locations around the globe.

Please advise if July 19 is good for you, if not, we can move this meeting to another time.

Best regards,

Scott

This memorandum was further proof I pursued acquiring Schunk. Other events that strengthened this conclusion were as follows: (1) prior to the Toronto meeting, I called Dave Quinn for his opinion about acquiring Schunk; (2) I contacted Morgan Crucible headquarters to let them know I was entering acquisition discussions; (3) I had a letter from the controller for Morgan AM&T–The Americas stating that the day following the Toronto meeting, I told him I was upset because I felt I'd been lured to Toronto under false pretenses; (4) the 1998 Morgan AM&T–The Americas long-range business plan showed Schunk was an acquisition target; and (5) a 1999 memo to the head of Acquisitions and Divestures at Morgan Crucible requested a meeting to go over details.

Yet in 2002 the U.S. government said I had not been interested in acquiring Schunk, but I had illegally shared prices and that's what the meetings were about. Again, the obvious was lost—why would I do such a thing after competing honestly and successfully in the marketplace for nearly thirty years?

One by one I responded to the demeaning accusations, not just by memory, but with memos, supporting witnesses, and with documents proving that my business performance ran contrary to the strategies of a cartel. None of it seemed to do any good. I didn't sense the kind of support from Tate and Levine that I expected and desperately needed.

By March 2003, I was working as president of Incon Lighting near Orlando, Florida, when Tate called. "Scott, it's a long shot, but we have one more option. You could go before the grand jury and plead your case. I can't be in there with you, but you can ask for a recess to consult with me," he told me.

"Good, I'm willing to give it a try," I responded.

I never heard another word from Tate about the grand jury. He later told me he was obligated to tell me I had the right to appear, but in his entire career, he never recommended any client do so. "It's just too risky," he said. "You're in a jury room with no one to defend you against an onslaught of questions from three or more prosecutors."

Tate also asked me if I'd take a polygraph test.

"Absolutely," I said. "And let's have Klatt, Massaro, and Floyd take one, too."

"Scott, they have immunity from prosecution," he replied. "Will you take it?" I told him I would.

Once again, nothing ever came of the proposal. The weeks, and my stomach, were slowly grinding. I think Tate had discussions with AUSA Rosenberg about my responses to Massaro, Klatt, and Floyd's testimonies, but I wasn't in the loop. Then, during July and August 2003, the words describing the government's charges against me began to change. The Justice Department had gone from *price fixing* to *pricing scheme*, and dangled a plea agreement for aiding and abetting. I believe Tate convinced Rosenberg that I would never plead guilty to price fixing.

I tried to figure out the government's strategy. The DOJ believed I fixed prices, but was charging me with aiding and abetting. I could only conclude they were afraid to put Massaro and Klatt on the witness stand. Tate also had concerns.

"I could handle Klatt, but Massaro's testimony would be a lethal body blow. He'll testify that he lied to Jim Younger initially."

I replied, "In all sincerity, Joe, Massaro told the truth until the documents he sent to Emerson surfaced with his fingerprints all over them. He had to get out of the mess somehow." Reality painfully sunk in: I was trapped by Massaro's guilt. He was off the hook, and I was just collateral damage.

Chapter 8
SENSIBLE BUT SEARING DECISIONS

Peace if possible, truth at all costs.[1]
—MARTIN LUTHER

As THE SUMMER OF 2003 MOVED ON, I HAD A SENSE OF RESOLUtion in front of me. I didn't like the way things looked, but the glimmer of light meant my family's anguish and heartache could end. I began to see three options before me:

- Negotiate a plea to an offense I did not commit and serve zero to six months in prison; no jail, halfway house, or monitor bracelet afterward.

- No plea, go to trial, and face not only price-fixing charges, but also obstruction of justice. The government made it clear it would hit me with everything. A guilty verdict could mean a forty-month sentence because the government contended my actions resulted in a one hundred million dollar commercial impact. Legal expenses, which wouldn't be covered by Morgan Crucible, could reach three million dollars.

- No plea, go to trial, and win.

I was ready to analyze and mull over these gut-wrenching possibilities alone, but Tate offered to come to Florida and meet with my family and friends. Hoping to protect the special people in my life from any more torment, I said it was a waste of time, but they all strongly wanted to ask questions and be part of the decision. Tate came to Florida, and it was clear the meeting would be much calmer if I weren't present. A close friend, Alan Norris, spent the day with me while Tate talked to Candy, my children, several close friends including Dave Quinn and Steve Salley, and my pastors.

The bottom line was that I had a 30 percent chance of winning at trial. Tate got a good taste of the loyalty and conviction among the people who knew me best. They believed in my innocence with every fiber of their being and were shocked to hear my chances at convincing a jury were so slim.

"Is there not one good man with integrity who will come forward and admit that Scott had nothing to do with this?" Candy anguished. "I just don't understand how the government justifies sending an innocent man to prison."

"They want to send a message," Tate answered.

That was not the answer Candy wanted to hear—that her husband, although innocent, would be punished to set an example for others. She left the room to compose herself. It was a very heated, emotional few hours as everyone faced up to the fact that my fate was essentially sealed. Aiding and abetting a crime was a level-twelve offense and my plea brought it down to a level-ten offense, which could qualify for home confinement or parole, but the government was set upon a prison sentence.

On the way back to the airport, Tate asked me if I had a home fax machine prior to moving to Florida.

"No. I made calls and sent faxes during the period under investigation from my Pure Carbon office in St. Marys." I figured after spending time with the people close to me, he may have actually been wondering if I did any of the things the government claimed.

Driving in the bright Florida sunshine, I reflected on the cold, snowy trip to my first interview at Pure Carbon in St. Marys nearly thirty years ago—it seemed like a hundred. I knew nothing about the company then, but it would become my challenge and passion. There was immense gratification in the successes I shared with dedicated colleagues. I was given the tremendous opportunity to work with Dave Quinn, a stellar businessman of sound character and integrity who remained a mentor and friend for my entire career. The years took twists and turns, and there were several moves and job changes, but Candy and I had dear friends in St. Marys, and they didn't believe any of the accusations against me. I didn't want those memories to turn bitter, but I could barely comprehend how I ended up facing such insane, distressing circumstances as a result of my decision to return to Pure Carbon in 1990.

The following week was decision time. I deliberated with Dave Quinn and two other highly respected friends who lived in St. Marys, Jim Ryan and Donny Flemming. They advised me to approach my quandary as I would a business decision. My heart wanted to fight on, but Morgan Crucible stripped me of my indemnification, so a trial could financially devastate my family.

I spent a lot of time in prayer and spoke to my pastor. After church that Sunday, I told Candy I was going to accept the government's plea proposal. I finally felt the Lord's presence and had peace about the decision. It's a good thing God protects us from knowing exactly what the future holds.

Joe Tate was surprised when I told him.

"My family and I have had enough hell—it has to end," I said.

"Scott, your testimony and attitude are consistent with a man who has told the truth," he countered. The show of support was welcomed. At that point, I'd finally convinced Joe of my innocence and his support raised my spirit. He then told me he was going to Washington to battle on my behalf. Had someone—anyone?—finally read my correspondence on the case, and decided the accusations against me didn't match my actions or the facts in my correspondence files? Maybe, just maybe, Tate had taken a further look at the statement Massaro made to Jim Younger before Sullivan and Cromwell produced the document Massaro sent to Emerson.

On July 16, 2003, I received an e-mail from Tate stating his office had been in contact with Washington. "Their position of six months is the best we're going to do," he said. "Although you already gave us authority to accept that deal, we wanted to fight some more, but we didn't get anywhere. Unless I hear from you to the contrary, I will call the Antitrust Division and accept the offer and move ahead quickly."

To this day, I still don't know who Tate was dealing with in Washington, but there was no turning back for me at this point, so I sent a reply e-mail: "I would like to thank you and Chris for your efforts on my behalf. Naturally, I am disappointed that the DOJ has not extended me the opportunity to explain my actions in this case."

My acceptance exploded when I received the first version of the plea agreement. I just couldn't sign my name to the document the way it was written. For example: "…the information will charge the defendant with corruptly persuading a witness to destroy documents relevant to an official proceeding in violation of 18 U.S.C. and U.S.C. 1512(b) (2) (B)."[2] The language was blatantly false, but the agreement said, "I would plead guilty to the criminal charge…and make a factual admission of guilt to the court." My friend Steve Salley said I would not only have to sign the plea, but appear before a federal judge and agree to the charges. I thought, "I have to lie to go to prison—what a system!"

Specific charges were defined by the Justice Department and when I read the language used to describe my actions, I saw red:

- I met with CC–1 [Massaro] on or about May 1999, and instructed him to destroy any documents that reflected any contacts with competitors. (*I made it clear to Tate that I had no recollection of any meeting with anyone in 1999 to destroy such documents. The only time I was remotely involved with any type of exercise to remove or destroy documents was during the years under Sam Parkhill with Stackpole, many years before 1999. He told everyone to stop collecting competitor price sheets, a forty-year practice that salespeople used to justify lowering Pure Carbon's prices. I followed Parkhill's directive and made sure all those lists were removed.*)

- On or about July 2001, I met with CC–1 [Massaro] and discussed, among other things, the grand jury's investigation into price fixing in the carbon industry, and encouraged him to destroy any documents that reflected contacts with competitors. (*This is simply false. No one ever disclosed to me that Morgan Crucible was served a subpoena in 1999 or that there was an ongoing grand*

> *jury investigation. I learned of the 1999 subpoena during a phone call from Dave Coker in October 2001, so there was no way I could have talked to Massaro about it. In July, I relayed Ian Norris's message about appearing on the government's radar and confronted Massaro as to whether anything illegal had taken place. He denied there was a problem, and I told him to just tell the truth.)*

- On or about August 2001, I caused CC–1 [Massaro] to destroy documents relevant to the Grand Jury investigation. *(Those documents probably could have helped my case, although I have no idea what was in them. How ironic—at the end of that conversation, I told Massaro, "Simply tell the truth if anyone ever asks you a question. I will never let you become a fall guy for Morgan Crucible.")*

I met with Massaro nearly two weeks before he says he destroyed his files in early August. I can only assume that someone else convinced him to destroy his files after I gave him the message from Norris. Once again, I believe the DOJ missed a lot. I told Tate I simply couldn't sign the first draft. He worked with the DOJ to change some of the language, and sent me a new draft of the plea agreement with changes:[3]

> Paragraph 2 (p. 2)—the staff has added 18 U.S.C and 2(a) which characterizes you as a "principal." This was added because of a compromise they made in the charge (which I will discuss next);

> Paragraph 4(c) has been changed from, "The defendant knowingly attempted to corruptly persuade an employee...to destroy" to "the defendant knowing aided and abetted...an employee to destroy." The latter language of "aiding and abetting" is a lesser offense than "attempting" and is closer to what happened since you were told that CC-1 had no documents to eliminate.

> Paragraph 4(c)(i) has been changed to reflect one competitor.

Paragraph 4(c)(ii) has been changed to delete "and encouraged him to destroy any documents that reflected any contacts with competitors."

Paragraph (4)(c)(iii) has been changed to add "due to his conversations," to reflect that you did not have a third conversation with CC-1. He then acted on his own.

Paragraph 8(a) has an addition insisted upon by the staff; "intermittent confinement" is not available as a substitute sentence. That is what they said all along.

In his e-mail, Tate added, "These language changes may sound a little better when we are before the court, and will permit you to acknowledge the facts in a more accurate fashion. Nevertheless, the [Antitrust] Division staff has not backed down on insisting on six months."

My days in prison were destined to be added to the DOJ tally for punishing individuals involved in cartels. Tate did say we could request a prison facility, and the Antitrust Division would support the recommendation to the court, but there was no guarantee the court or Bureau of Prisons would accede to our request.

"Finally, I have asked the staff for a date for an interview if we decide that it makes sense for you to tell your side of the story," Tate continued. "They have said they will meet if we so request, but it will not change their ideas or the plea bargain. They intend to file the information on September 2, 3, or 4. They will get back to me on that."

On August 13, 2003, I e-mailed Tate, "The language changes reflected in the amended plea agreement dated August 6, 2003, while an improvement, do not accurately reflect my conversation with Massaro and I cannot sign a document that would perjure myself before God and a federal judge. Martin Luther wrote, 'Peace if possible, truth at all costs.' Joe, I desire peace in my life, but not at the cost of the truth."

Candy consoled me, desperate to put an end to the hurt and frustration.

"Yes, you have to appear before this earthly judge and admit to something you know is false," she said. "But our heavenly Father is the ultimate

Judge, and He knows your heart and why you're making this sacrifice. He's the only Judge we really care about."

She was right. The next day I had a lengthy phone call with Tate and then sent him another e-mail, "First and foremost, do you feel the language in the government's plea agreement is fair to me? It is very difficult for me to accept the language given the fact that Massaro told me he had no documents when I questioned him. Joe, this is a difficult process. Simply negotiate the best language you can and I will sign the plea agreement ending this tragedy. I will not subject my family to any further suffering. I am at peace with myself knowing God knows that I had nothing to do with price fixing, a *pricing scheme*, or any knowledge of the documents Massaro had or destroyed. Joe, let's move on. You have convinced me that nothing is going to change. I must still insist that I have the opportunity to meet with the Justice Department. I want the truth to be known, even if it falls on deaf ears."

On August 20, AUSA McClain sent Tate the final plea agreement, saying it had to be approved by Washington. "They" hadn't yet reviewed the documents. Again, I wondered, who was "Washington" specifically? Did "Washington" have an actual name? Tate forwarded the agreement to me that afternoon.

"I have made every effort to bring them as close to what you recall of your conversations with Massaro," Tate wrote. "This is all I can do. Believe me, I have tried, but they say this is his version. I recommend we live with it and tell the judge (when called to do so) that the events took place even if your recollection of the words may differ somewhat from Massaro. I am trying to arrange a meeting for you with the Division staff attorneys on September 3 or 4."

The DOJ also asked if I would give them an affidavit of my conversations with Ian Norris regarding the documents, although I wouldn't benefit by cooperating. I declined.

The plea was scheduled to be submitted to Washington on September 10. I contacted Dave Quinn and asked him to join me in Philadelphia on September 4. I hoped there wouldn't be a problem with him sitting in—obviously I was growing somewhat paranoid given the ordeal of the past two years.

The format for the meeting was interesting. My attorney, Joe Tate, would ask questions, and then the DOJ attorneys could ask follow-up questions. I knew the hearing wouldn't change anything—I was going to prison—but it was my chance to tell my side of the story, and I wasn't going to give it up.

We arrived at the Curtis Building in Philadelphia at 2:15 that afternoon. Assistant U.S. Attorneys McClain and Rosenberg were joined by the FBI agent who delivered my subpoena that pleasant August afternoon nearly two years prior. I sat in the middle chair on one side of a conference table, Quinn was to my left, and Tate was seated at my right. Directly across table in the middle chair was AUSA McClain, Rosenberg sat to her right, and the FBI agent was on her left. I looked directly into McClain's eyes and realized this was one tough lady when the occasion necessitated. The room was tense, but I was anxious for her to hear me out. I had no expectations about the outcome. I began by stating that I knew what I said that day could be used against me in a court of law, but I was there voluntarily to answer all questions fully and honestly.

Tate and I had never discussed what he would ask, but his first question was perfect: what did you do when you took over Europe? It was my chance to repudiate the Justice Department's claims that I was a member of the cartel, an insider, someone who went along to get along. I fully explained the series of events that led to my firing Laurence Bryce, even though Ian Norris reinstated him in another capacity. Pure Carbon Company achieved steady sales growth in Europe in the 1970s, 80s, and early 90s, but sales crashed after Morgan Crucible's acquisition and Bryce took over managing Morgan AM&T–Europe. Having spent considerable time in Europe developing new business for the Pure Carbon Company, I was aware of the competitive advantages Morgan AM&T had in the marketplace, so I was mystified as to why sales were evaporating.

Prior to the Morgan Crucible acquisition, Laurence Bryce and I had worked together at Pure Carbon Company and he was my direct report, so I attempted to refocus and invigorate him and his team on moving forward and capitalizing on new business opportunities. I moved slowly at first by familiarizing myself with the management and customer service issues that I thought were contributing to the negative performance. I sent Bryce and his team a series of memoranda that specifically addressed issues related to the financial forecast for the business, new business development efforts, continuous cost-reduction initiatives, and customer service issues. There was little data available as to what was causing the decline, by then in its fourth year, and I had to take a more active role identifying and addressing the root causes of the problems.

The deterioration in Europe continued, and I sent Bryce a comprehensive memorandum, "The Way Forward—Europe," in early 1999. It expressed my concerns about the overall performance of Morgan AM&T's European business, past organizational moves by Bryce, the lack of new business development, and the fact that Morgan AM&T–Europe didn't have an application engineering department driving those efforts. This fact alone was alarming since application engineering was a core competency at Morgan AM&T and was critical to the success we were experiencing in the United States.

Because the management reporting systems at Morgan AM&T–Europe were weak or non-existent, I asked my colleague Floyd Gerber, former vice president of sales for Pure Carbon and Morgan AM&T–The Americas, to institute necessary changes to stabilize and refocus our marketing and sales efforts in Europe. Gerber and his wife moved to the Gosport area in England, and he was instrumental in incorporating changes that produced significant improvements. In addition, I promoted Simon Hussey to vice president of operations for Europe, moving him from our Graflon Division in Houston, Texas, to our Gosport facility. Hussey was an excellent addition to our European management team, and his performance far exceeded my expectations. At the same time, I rehired John Herke as vice president of sales for Morgan AM&T–Europe. He was a very intelligent, highly motivated manager who previously worked for Morgan Crucible, but left the company because of Bryce. Herke also made an immediate impact, and his market knowledge in both carbon and silicon carbide proved to be a winning combination.

I continued by explaining to AUSA McClain what happened at the Focus Accounts Review meeting in Gosport. I stated that Bryce's presentation was contrived, and I told my colleague, Everett Chorney, if Bryce asks you about his status, tell him to find a job, I'm going to replace him. In response, Bill Macfarlane called and told me to reinstate Bryce at Ian Norris's insistence, and I threatened to resign. I had decided to run Europe myself until the business was stabilized. Norris moved Bryce to another position within the company.

One thing I failed to tell the Justice Department that day was that Andy McIntosh, the head of Morgan Crucible's Human Resources Department, had called me in to discuss the issues concerning Bryce. Obviously someone had solicited McIntosh's assistance in resolving our contentious relationship. The outcome was a job description that defined Bryce's responsibilities and authority in Europe. Regrettably, it had little effect on Bryce's overall performance, and his failure to meet those requirements ultimately led me to terminate his services. I would later learn that McIntosh knew all about the cartel! Here again—how interesting.

I described for the DOJ representatives the low-cost operations I established in Hungary, the addition of salespeople and application engineers for the German market, and how I set up an outside board of directors to oversee our progress and changes in Europe. We started tracking on-time deliveries, tackled scrap issues, and consolidated orders in some of our plants for more efficiency. When Ian Norris requested a progress report in a meeting at Gosport before the Morgan Crucible Executive Committee in April 2000, I was ready with charts and graphs that reflected steady improvement in cost reduction and profitability after years of significant decline. I put the presentation together on very short notice. I had been documenting all the progress the new team was making and reflected the changes in a series of graphs showing the status of orders, sales, and profits for the four-year period prior to April 2000, and our projections going forward.

At one point during my explanation, McClain interrupted me and said I had a tremendous reputation. She stated everyone she had spoken with had positive remarks to offer. Needless to say, I was a bit surprised to receive the compliment, but it speaks to McClain's fairness.

After this summary, Tate asked me about my involvement with Jim Floyd at Schunk regarding Borg Warner Industrial Products (BWIP) and John Crane–Canada. I explained in detail my conversation and actions regarding these companies. I was simply trying to help a "friend" save his job. I wondered if anyone had asked Floyd what he was doing for me in exchange for my supposedly illegal assistance to him. To my knowledge, Schunk never sold any products to BWIP or John Crane–Canada as a direct result of any conversations I had with Floyd. My discussions with Floyd centered on his requests for assistance in order to convince these customers to test Schunk's materials and his desire to persuade Schunk's management to make a capital investment for equipment to machine silicon carbide.

I added that about the same time Floyd asked for help getting Schunk's materials tested at BWIP, Morgan AM&T–Europe's sales manager, Edye Thein, was applying pressure through my boss, Roy Waldheger, to get me to raise prices on products we sold BWIP in Europe and the United States. I refused, and the history of those discussions is in my files. If I wouldn't change pricing at the request of managers in my own company, why on earth would I entertain setting prices with Floyd or anyone else? In addition, I adamantly refused Floyd's request to withdraw or change prices to Owens Corning Fiberglass, an account Morgan AM&T took from Schunk, and told Floyd not to call me again. Morgan AM&T received the first contract in January 1996 and renewed it every year through 2000, my last year as company president. I noticed the Justice Department officials were taking a lot of notes when I made this statement.

Rosenberg wanted to know how I could explain prices on two families of parts at John Crane increasing 10 percent after the meeting in Toronto with Schunk.

"I can't explain it," I said. "I'm not aware of any price increases at John Crane in the last ten years, only those associated with quantity changes initiated by Crane."

McClain then asked about a script I was supposed to have been given to follow in case I was ever questioned by the Justice Department.

"I have never seen a script, not one single word." The idea that a script existed was appalling. I agreed that anyone involved in such a meeting should be prosecuted, but I knew nothing about it. Who was that one particular American who received it? And approved it? Why wasn't this person identified and prosecuted?

I told the group there was an obvious disconnect between what others had said and my testimony, and I requested a polygraph test. Nobody responded. I wondered if they even wanted the truth.

By the close of the meeting I was drained. Someone touched my elbow as I stood to leave, and I assumed it was Quinn, but it was McClain. "Scott, you're a courageous man," she said.

I'm not sure I felt brave, but a weight lifted from my shoulders. The emotional pressure of the past two years had unleashed. Twice during the proceeding I had to leave the room and compose myself; upon returning one time, Quinn was telling the assembled group I deserved a medal for taking on the cartel. Conflicting emotions rushed through me that day—fear, anger, relief—but I knew my reputation was at stake, and I couldn't go quietly into the night.

Tate, Quinn, and I had coffee afterward in the basement floor of the Curtis Federal Office Building.

"Scotty, I think you hit a homerun," Quinn said.

"My heart is on the floor in there," I sighed.

Tate agreed I did an outstanding job, but, ever the realist, reminded me that nothing would change. Joe was right, as usual.

> As water reflects a face, so a man's heart reflects the man.
> —PROVERBS 27:19

I can't fully describe my feelings sitting on the plane headed home that night. Over the course of the two-year struggle, I frequently found myself stopping by my church at various times of the day, as if drawn by a magnet. I'd sit in the sanctuary and quietly share my burden with the Lord. It was about the only time I could let out a deep breath and just rest in God's grace. That peace—that surpasseth understanding—was with me on my flight home from Philadelphia.

Chapter 9
A PLEA FOR JUSTICE

SIX DAYS AFTER MY MEETING WITH THE DOJ, MY ATTORNEY, JOE Tate, called and said nothing had changed—I was going to prison. "I'll get back to you as soon as I get the sentencing date," he said. I still disagreed with the language in the fourth version (!) of my plea agreement, but Tate told me it was "as good as it gets."

I signed it.

Tate said it was possible to speed up the sentencing process by waiving the standard pre-sentence investigation report (PSI). I did so in order to proceed immediately to the sentencing hearing. I was ready to serve my six-month sentence and move on with my life. In a later conversation with Tate, he advised me to hire an outside agency to prepare my PSI, since the sentencing hearing wasn't scheduled until November 24, 2003, before Federal Judge Anita Brody.

We'd been told to request a federal prison of our choice, but there was no guarantee the judge would comply. We asked for the federal prison camp located at Eglin Air Force Base in the Florida Panhandle. I just wanted to serve my time and get on with my life.

The night before the court appearance, Candy and I arrived at the hotel in Philadelphia accompanied by Candy's brother, Greg, Dave Quinn, and Larry Thorwart, vice president of Morgan AM&T who was a family friend and trusted colleague. Candy, Greg, and I met Tate that afternoon to prepare for the hearing, and we learned the judge had moved up my appearance to nine o'clock that morning because she wanted more time. Tate was curious about the move because a trusted confidante had gone over my file and felt something just didn't add up. Later I learned that confidante was Joe's wife.

I thought maybe the judge was influenced by the many letters to the court from family and friends, and one in particular from my pastor:

Dear Judge Brody:

I am the Rector of St. Peter's Episcopal Church. I am writing as an advocate for one of my parishioners, Mr. Scott Brown. I have been his priest for the past five years.

I believe the U.S. government is unjustly forcing him into a no-win legal situation.

Every bone in my body tells me that Scott Brown is a man of integrity and honesty. I know him to be a person with a deep Christian faith, a man with a deep love for his country. In my mind, he represents everything that is great about the United States and its citizens. It is heart wrenching for our church community to see such a well respected and great man be humiliated by the U.S. government.

He is an outstanding citizen who generously contributes to his church and community. He had donated his time to building our youth program and school. He has given generously to the support of our Honduras outreach and mission trips. He has fed the homeless with us.

Scott was responsible for building Berwind Park [St. Marys, PA], a million dollar state-of-the-art baseball field. Scott was also instrumental in building the girls' softball field for St. Marys area high school. He was the high school football coach and donated every penny of his salary back to the school's athletic program, and spent thousands of dollars of his own money to upgrade the team equipment and field. Scott was awarded the 1999 Pennsylvania American Legion Distinguished Service Award and was inducted into the American Legion Baseball Hall of Fame for his work in the community and state. That community offered to name Berwind Park after him—but he declined the honor!

This is not a greedy man!

I know that it is important to root out corporate corruption in the wake of recent corporate scandals. However, it is very possible that in the government's zeal to prosecute criminals there are occasions in which it might prosecute the innocent. In this case, the government is prosecuting one of the good guys. Scott was one of those instrumental in cleaning up corporate corruption in his own company. Presently, Scott Brown is being persecuted with a philosophy of guilty until proven innocent. He is being forced to accept a plea under threat of an expensive trial and lengthy jail time. He is an innocent man being used as the scapegoat for Morgan and the U.S. government. To this point, there has been no justice.

I can no longer watch a good man be unjustly prosecuted by the country that he loves. We live in a great and powerful country, but must be humble with that great power. I am humbly asking the U.S. justice system to let one of my people go.

If there is one man worth being an advocate for—here he is! You are an honorable judge—that is your title—do not allow this miscarriage of justice.

I am faithfully yours,
Reverend Charles L. Holt

Reverend Holt's letter was quite moving. In fact, after reading all the letters to the court from friends, family, and colleagues, Candy said it must have felt like I was experiencing my own eulogy. The support and sincerity were true blessings, but I knew my fate was sealed.

The next morning, my primary concern was remaining calm and focused enough to get through the plea and sentencing hearing. It was a damp and cold Philadelphia day, but my arthritic knees and a heavy heart put me in a sweat during the walk from the Marriott Hotel to the Federal courthouse. United States Assistant Attorneys McClain and Rosenberg arrived, and then Judge Brody took the bench.[1]

* * * *

"Good morning, Mr. Brown."

I was sworn in: "Do you understand that you're now under oath and if you answer any question falsely, your answer could later be used against you in a prosecution for perjury or making false statements? You have to say yes or no."

"Yes, ma'am. I understand."

Judge Brody proceeded through more opening formalities, and then asked, "Did your lawyer explain the written plea agreement to you?"

"Yes, your honor. He did"

"All right. Has your lawyer so far done everything that you wished him to do?"

"Yes, your honor, he has."

Assistant U.S. Attorney Rosenberg summed up the plea agreement:

"The government and Mr. Brown have agreed that an appropriate sentence in this case is six months of incarceration with no substitution confinement, a fine of twenty thousand dollars, and no period of supervised release. Mr. Brown will also be required to pay one hundred dollars special assessment. If the plea is accepted, the government has agreed it will not bring any further charges against Mr. Brown for any offense committed prior to the plea agreement involving the sale of mechanical or electrical carbon products that was related to an antitrust conspiracy or an investigation of such a conspiracy."

Agreed with the terms of the plea... not in my heart, but to get my life back. Judge Brody looked at me.

"Do you agree that these are the terms of the plea agreement? Do you agree, Mr. Brown?" Brody asked.

"Yes, your honor. I do."

"All right. Are there... other than those terms, did anyone promise or offer you anything else to get you to plead guilty?"

"No, ma'am. They did not."

"All right. Do you understand... I'll receive the plea agreement? Do you understand that no one can guarantee you what sentence you will get from me?"

"Yes, your honor. I do."

"I can refuse to accept, and then you have the right to withdraw your pleas. Do you understand that?"

"Yes, your honor, I do."

"Are you doing this of your own free will?"

"Yes, I am, your honor."

"Did anyone tell you what to say today or put words in your mouth, so to speak?"

"No, your honor."

"Do you understand that you're entering a plea to a felony, and you will be judged guilty of a felony, which may deprive you of valuable civil rights such as the right to vote, hold public office, serve on a jury, possess a firearm, or hold a professional license?"

"Yes, your honor, I do."

Then Judge Brody went over the consequences of forfeiting a trial: I gave up the right to confront and cross-examine the government's witnesses against me; a twelve-member jury would have to unanimously vote for guilt, and I could appeal to a higher court if found guilty; in a trial, I wouldn't have to testify. With every ounce of my being, I wanted Klatt, Massaro, Emerson, and Floyd on the stand, but it would have cost a fortune, and the tragedy had to end.

Judge Brody addressed the government's attorneys.

"All right. Please state the maximum and minimum terms."

"Certainly, your honor," Rosenberg said. "The maximum penalty for this crime is ten years imprisonment, two hundred fifty thousand dollar fine, and three years with supervised release."

"Tell me how you calculated the sentence."

"Certainly, your honor. Well, first, let me say that the current sentencing guidelines have been amended that the penalty is more severe than it was at the time when the offense was committed. Therefore, at the time it was committed, the base offense level was twelve. There are no additional aggravating factors. We believe Mr. Brown has accepted responsibility entitling him to a decrease of two, which results in an offense level of ten. The guidelines range for an offense level ten is six to twelve months."

Rosenberg went on to explain that our agreement was based on a period of confinement, with no option for alternative confinement. Judge Brody asked about the fine.

"We've agreed to a twenty thousand dollar fine."

"Twenty thousand dollars. Okay. All right. Do you understand those guideline ranges," she asked me.

"Yes, your honor. I do."

I had previously said I would pay the fine on the day of my appearance, if possible, and I paid for a pre-sentencing investigative report, required by the Bureau of Prisons, instead of waiting for it to get through governmental bureaucratic processing. I prayed, "Please, God, just let this end."

Judge Brody fully explained that the plea agreement limited my right to appeal and undertake other legal actions, and, again, she explained what my rights were regarding a trial. Then AUSA Rosenberg presented the charge.

The defendant knowingly corruptly persuaded or induced another person to destroy or conceal documents, and second, that at the time, caused or induced another person to destroy or conceal documents, and he did so intending to impair the document's integrity or availability for use in official proceeding. In this case, Mr. Brown is not charged with doing these acts himself but aiding and abetting those acts, and for the defendant to be found guilty of aiding or abetting, it's not necessarily that he personally commit the acts constituting the crime as long as someone committed the crime and the defendant knowingly and intentionally did an act constituting a substantial step towards the commission of the crime.

"Do you understand these elements of your crime?" Judge Brody asked.

"Yes, your honor."

Rosenberg continued.

In both April 1999, and in August, 2001, a federal grand jury sitting in the eastern district of Pennsylvania issued subpoenas duces tecum to Morganite Industries, Inc. in connection with an antitrust investigation of the carbon products industry.

The scope of those subpoenas covered Morganite Industries' subsidiaries and affiliates, among those a company called Morgan Advanced Materials and Technology. Mr. Brown was an officer of Morgan Advanced Materials and Technology at the time of the first subpoena, and he was a consultant on the board of directors at the time of the second subpoena.

Some time around May 1999, Mr. Brown met with an officer of Morganite's parent company, the Morgan Crucible Company, who instructed Mr. Brown to make certain that a specific employee of Morgan Advanced Materials had no documents in his files reflecting contacts with competitors. The employee was Mr. Brown's subordinate, and at the time that employee did in fact have contact with competitors regarding pricing.

Mr. Brown later relayed the message from his superior at Morgan Crucible to his subordinate how he should have no documents reflecting contacts with competitors in his files. At the time, the employee did not believe he had any such files and took no action.

Sometime around July 2001, Mr. Brown again met with his subordinate and discussed the grand jury's investigation of the carbon product's industry. Soon after that conversation while looking for documents in response to the August 2001 subpoena, Mr. Brown's subordinate found documents that were relevant to the grand jury investigation that related to the contacts with competitors. With the conversations with Mr. Brown in mind, that subordinate destroyed those documents, making them unavailable to the Grand Jury.

> Many seek an audience with a ruler, but it is from the LORD that man gets justice.
>
> —PROVERBS 29:26

Judge Brody then asked the piercing question, "Do you fully admit to these facts?"

I tried to contain my words and emotions. "I would like to explain myself, your honor."

"Well, do you want to explain yourself now or do you want to explain yourself before I sentence you? Talk to your lawyer."

Tate jumped in. "I think, your honor, Mr. Brown can give an answer to your question."

"All right. I want to find out whether or not he admits to the facts."

"I do admit to one fact, your honor—"

"Well, what fact is that?" she cut in.

"I cannot recall a date in '99, number one, but I can say unequivocally that I was at Morgan Crucible sometime I believe in the year 2000 walking by the CEO's desk when he hollered at me to tell Laurence and Tony to get rid of any documents they have."

"Is that your subordinate?" Brody asked.

"Mr. Massaro was, but at that time Mr. Bryce wasn't because I terminated his employment, so I did nothing because Bryce didn't work for me, and 'Tony' could have been one of two people. I dropped it—I didn't do anything.

"I believe it was early July 2001, prior to the company picnic in St.

Marys, Pennsylvania, I got a call from the CEO again, Ian Norris, telling me it's imperative that I get to Tony and tell him that he's going to appear on the government's radar, and tell him to get rid of any documents he has. In all sincerity, your honor, it scared the living hell out of me because I didn't know he had any documents."

I really wasn't prepared to state my case, but I wasn't going to stop, even though I figured Tate and Rosenberg were cringing.

"I called Massaro and told him I was coming up there and insisted he meet with me for a heart-to-heart. I asked him two questions: did you ever fix prices I'm not aware of, and do you have any documents I should be concerned about? He said no, and that he didn't know why Norris was concerned.

"That's what happened, your honor, but when it happened, I didn't think I was breaking the law. That's my dilemma. I can't tell it any other way."

"Go back again," Judge Brody said, "because I'm not sure that I believe it is breaking the law. So let's go back, because I have to find a factual basis for your plea."

Rosenberg interrupted, "Your honor, if this case were to go to trial, there would be substantial evidence that Mr. Brown did know that there was an anti-trust conspiracy at the time, although we understand Mr. Brown does not believe that."

"Well...he's unwilling to admit that he knew it. I'm not sure I can accept a plea if he says he doesn't have any knowledge of a conspiracy and he goes in and he talks to somebody and says to this person 'Do you have any papers?' That's what he did, is that correct? Is that what your claim is?" Judge Brody asked me.

I said, "I asked him if he ever set a price; he said no. I asked him if he had any documents; he said no. I asked, why is Norris saying you're going to appear on the government's radar? He said he didn't know. That's what happened. I delivered the message. The other point is I just don't recall anything in 1999."

"Well, I'll tell you what I'm going to do," Brody said, "I'm not going to sentence you today. I know it's not a happy situation, but I can't take a plea that I have a real feeling about that you may not be guilty and that there may not be a factual basis to. I mean, that's a very serious issue from a court's point of view.

"I'll give you a few minutes to talk to your lawyer about whether your want to go forward, but I cannot in good conscience accept your plea if I don't believe you're guilty."

Tate spoke up.

"Your honor, I talked to Mr. Brown about exactly this. He knows the evidence is overwhelming. The government and these two prosecutors and I have worked on this matter for many months. Mr. Brown feels that with hindsight, what he said and the way he said it to Mr. Massaro, Tony... he delivered the message."

I knew I had to accept my attorney's position, but it tore me apart. If I believed the evidence was overwhelming, truthful, and accurate, I would have been down on my knees thanking the Lord for only six months in prison—instead I fought the charges for more than two years.

"I have to hear it from him," Brody said.

At that point, Judge Brody granted Tate permission to question me.

"When you talked to Tony Massaro, did you know there was a grand jury investigation?"

"No, I did not."

"At the time you talked to Mr. Norris, did he in any way indicate to you that there had been subpoenas?"

"No," I answered, "He's never said that."

"When did you receive your subpoena?"

"August 6, 2001."

"And you're telling the court that prior to that, you did not know of any subpoena?"

"Absolutely. That's what I'm saying."

"At the time you talked to Mr. Massaro, did you know Mr. Norris was worried about documents that might be in possession of Tony Massaro?" Tate asked.

"Definitely from the conversation. Yes sir."

"And that Mr. Norris wanted you to tell Mr. Massaro to get rid of those documents."

"Definitely."

"Is there any doubt in your mind as we sit here today that Mr. Massaro got that exact message from you that Norris wanted him to get rid of documents."

"Definitely, that's the message he got. That's true, your honor," I said.

Judge Brody remained hesitant. "So what you're really saying is that the government can prove its case, but you don't believe that its case is correct. Is that basically what you're saying? That's the bottom line—do you want me to accept the plea?"

I'm not sure who was backed into a corner at this point—I guess we all were. Rosenberg reiterated that the government had overwhelming evidence against me. Judge Brody pressed me about going to trial unless I believed the government could prove its case beyond reasonable doubt. Candy just held hands with the two people sitting next to her and whispered, "Jesus, Jesus. Jesus..." The tension and emotion were palpable.

"You see it on TV, but sitting there experiencing it was excruciating," Candy later said. "I knew you were dying inside, and I was just torn apart—part of me hoped the judge wouldn't believe you were guilty and we'd go to trial, and the other half just wanted our pain to end."

I struggled for the right words to answer Judge Brody. "I believe, your honor, when I gave Mr. Massaro the message, I broke the law, and I fully accept responsibility for that."

"I didn't ask you that question," Brody said, "I asked you whether or not you believe that the government can prove what it says it can prove, even though you may not believe it's true."

"Your honor, I really don't know. You want an honest answer...I don't know."

"Well, why are you pleading?"

"Because, your honor, it's been more than two years. I haven't slept more than two hours a night for two years. I need to move on with my life. I don't want to go through another year or two. I may not even be here the way I'm going. I want this behind me."

Tate then requested a break, and Judge Brody insisted on only five minutes.

"You're blowing this, Scott," he blurted. "If you persist, the judge is going to throw out the case and you'll have to go to trial."

"I'm simply telling the truth." What I couldn't tell Judge Brody was that Morgan Crucible reneged on their pledge to pay my legal fees if I went to trial, and the cost would run as high as three million dollars. I had to sit on my thumbs.

After the five-minute break, and back on record, Brody asked me if I believed the government could prove beyond reasonable doubt that I was guilty as charged.

"Yes, your honor."

"Are you sure of that."

"Yes, your honor."

"I'm very concerned about somebody in my courtroom pleading guilty when they truly believe they're not. That's very difficult. But we all live in this world, and if the government can prove it, after all, there's certain facts in 1999 you don't remember."

"Uh huh."

"So you understand I have a great deal of concern, and knowing my concern, do you still want to plead guilty?"

"Yes, your honor. I do appreciate your concerns."

Judge Brody asked if I understood I had the right to a grand jury that would determine if there was probable cause to indict me. I said I voluntarily waived that right.

I was then formally charged by the court.

"I plead guilty," I said.

"All right," Judge Brody said. "I will sentence you today…do you want to be heard? You have an absolute right to be heard."

"Yes. I have a short statement."

I needed to compose myself, and Tate interjected. "Your honor, it might be better if I spoke on Mr. Brown's behalf."

"Just relax a little bit," Brody said to me. "I want to hear from you. I really do."

In the meantime Tate referred to letters to the court from my immediate family, Dave Quinn, and other associates testifying to my integrity and devotion to my family.

"It is a very humbling experience," Tate said. "He has made a mistake. He has admitted the mistake to the government, to you, and to his God.

With that, we ask you to sentence him in accordance with the plea bargain and to recommend to the Bureau of Prisons that he serve his time at Eglin Air Force Base."

I was ready to speak.

"Good morning, your honor, Judge Brody. In the name of the Father, the Son, and the Holy Spirit, thank you Lord for all the blessings you have given me and my family. You have bountifully blessed my life with a wonderful wife, children, and two great sons-in-law.

"Today I accept full responsibility for any action on my part that has broken the law of our country. I stand ready to serve the sentence your honor imposes, and I will strive to be a model prisoner during my incarceration." I concluded by asking for a facility close to my family in Florida.

Judge Brody accepted my statement and plea. She then added one thing more, telling me to somehow use my experience to help others.

"My experience in eleven years in federal court has taught me how important this is, and there are many, many businessmen who are of really decent spirit who have broken the law. So when you leave prison, my strong suggestion is that you help the SEC and your colleagues, and tell your colleagues just what can happen if you're not absolutely clear about this issue... you cannot obstruct justice, and you cannot come to a price agreement with anybody. If you want to do something that's really valuable to you and your fellow man, that's what you can do, and that would be really serving the needs of your country and your colleagues."

"That's great advice, your honor," I said.

"Please stand. Now, this twenty-fourth day of November, the year 2003, in the matter of the United States versus F. Scott Brown, criminal action 3–628, I sentence you to six months imprisonment and a twenty thousand dollar fine to be paid forthwith... and a one hundred dollar special assessment, no supervised release to follow, and other terms or conditions."

* * * *

That was it. Judge Brody said she would urge the Bureau of Prisons to assign me to Eglin Air Force Base. I would report after Christmas, on January 12, 2004.

Following the proceeding, AUSA Rosenberg came over and patted my attorney Tate on the back, congratulating him on a job well done, which disturbed my family and friends. The FBI agent led me through processing with the U.S. Marshall and FBI, while Tate tied up loose ends and then left the building. Again, my small group of supporters wondered about his cool distance that day. I figured Tate had done his job, part of which meant keeping an emotional distance from a client's family, and it was time to move on to Joe's next case.

I was put on edge again when a U.S. Marshall threatened to incarcerate me on the spot because my paperwork hadn't arrived from the court, which is necessary prior to being photographed and fingerprinted. When the FBI agent intervened on my behalf, the officer told him to sit down and shut up. The agent stayed with me for the processing by the federal marshal, and then walked with me to meet my family and friends. Before leaving, he put his arm around my shoulder and said that after more than thirty years he was retiring and that he felt it could not come fast enough. To this day I wonder what was really going through his mind.

Candy and I returned to the hotel to pack and head home. I once again had peace. Candy suggested we spend time on the flight preparing for our next Bible study class. We were struck by the first verse on our assignment list; it was from the Book of Matthew (2:6), "True instruction was in his mouth and nothing false was found on his lips." Immensely touched, we thanked God for the gift of His Word. I had prayed to just tell the truth that day, and I did. Then Candy turned to me with tears in her eyes.

"I made a mistake—it was supposed to be Matthew 2:6, but I looked up Malachi 2:6."

It wasn't a mistake—the Holy Spirit was holding our hands and guiding our actions. God not only walked with us, but carried the burden.

I received notice a few weeks later that I'd be going to Eglin Federal Prison Camp in the Florida Panhandle, near Fort Walton Beach, as federal prison inmate 57918–066. I began a daily regimen of prayer and Bible study, but hidden from me was exactly how the Lord would incredibly deliver me during those six months.

But I call to God, and the Lord saves me. Evening, morning and noon I cry out in distress, and he hears my voice, He ransoms me unharmed from the battle waged against me, even though many oppose me.

—PSALM 55:16–18

Chapter 10
CONFINED, BUT RELEASED

GLIN FEDERAL PRISON CAMP HAS A STORIED PAST INCLUDING the Nixon years and the infamous Watergate break-in. Several of President Nixon's staff served time at Eglin; one dorm was built just for them. There are rumors about their special treatment—an upgraded menu and weekend releases—but those privileges didn't apply when I got there. The camp doesn't have walls or barbed wire fences, but simply a yellow line that marks its boundary. The eight hundred inmates are assigned to maintaining the grounds and buildings at the airbase, giving them time outdoors and contact with civilians and military personnel.

January 11 loomed constantly over my loved ones and me, and then arrived too fast. My family and I stood in the kitchen and hugged and cried. I asked my son, Rick, and son-in-law, Greg, to drive me to the airport and spare Candy a public scene. She trembled as we said good-bye.

"Don't worry, I will handle this," I said.

"I don't want to go down a slope of self-pity," Candy said. "I know Satan wants to use fear against us."

At the airport, Rick walked me to the gate and we hugged again. He's as strong as an ox and breaking his grip wasn't easy. I abruptly turned and walked away—I couldn't look back. Waiting for the boarding call, I opened my Bible. "In the beginning..." I was going to read it from cover to cover during my incarceration.

I had called a longtime friend, Chip Holcombe, who lived in Ft. Walton Beach to pick me up at the airport. He and I dined together that night and reminisced about how we met. Chip was a store manager for Edwin Watts Golf, and Pure Carbon Company and Morgan AM&T were customers. We grew to be friends and remained in touch, and here was God's providence again: he knew people who worked at Eglin. "You'll do fine in there," he said. We met again the following morning, and I ate what I knew would be my last extravagant breakfast for a while. Chip assured me that he knew of safe and reasonable accommodations for my family. I didn't tell him I'd instructed Candy not to visit me while I was in prison.

Inmates are only allowed to bring a Bible, glasses or dentures, and a wedding band if it conforms to regulations. Normally within the first few weeks of incarceration, new inmates are permitted to deposit three hundred dollars into a commissary account to purchase phone time (a maximum of fifteen minutes a day, up to three hundred minutes a month), food, clothing, and boots or tennis shoes. During my six months at Eglin, I came across several prisoners who had absolutely no outside financial support and their only means to purchase anything was what they earned from their camp job assignment, which paid an average of fourteen cents per hour.

I arrived early for my check-in so I could get used to my surroundings. Once inside the Prison Camp Administration Building, I had my picture taken and was fingerprinted. The officer who processed me was friendly, and after the first shot, said, "Is this the way you want to be remembered? Let's do it again with a smile." I then had to peel down for a strip search, which took only seconds, and handed over the clothing I wore that day to be put in a box and shipped home. I was issued a pair of slacks, a white T-shirt, white socks, underwear, and sandals, which were later replaced with work clothes resembling army fatigues and work boots. The Bureau of Prisons issues disposable razors, a toothbrush, and toothpaste. Nobody is allowed to have shaving cream in a can—somewhere in the system an ingenious prisoner turned one into a makeshift bomb.

Every inmate gets a federal prison ID number with a picture, and it must be on your person at all times, except when sleeping. The number is printed on your clothing and is necessary for commissary purchases.

Once my processing was complete, I was instructed to take a seat in a small holding area. Then I waited...and waited, for hours. Sitting there with nothing to do, I thought about the fleeting moments when I thought my nightmare was over: when Morgan Crucible's law firm, Pillsbury Winthrop, reported that after reviewing thousands of documents, they found no evidence of price fixing of mechanical carbon products;

when the company's second law firm, Sullivan and Cromwell, reported that Schunk's claims that I participated in price fixing were false; and, finally, the numerous calls from Ian Norris and David Coker telling me not to worry, that the whole thing was about electrical carbon and had nothing to do with me. There was great elation in the Brown household on those occasions—now I sat in a prison cell.

The processing officer returned. He said he had bad news for me. I panicked, fearing something had happened to my wife or a member of our family. It turned out my pre-sentence paperwork didn't arrive, so they could not take me in that day. As a result, they had to send me to Santa Rosa County Jail near Pensacola until it arrived. I offered to have Candy fax a copy of the PSI report, but it had to come from the Bureau of Prisons. It was three o'clock in the afternoon—I had been there six hours and I was still in the holding cell, which had a large steel door, a window to look through, a toilet, and sink. My thoughts drifted to Candy and how I could let her know what was happening. More hours passed. Another shift of officers arrived and moved me to another room. It had been nearly eight weeks since my court appearance and Eglin still didn't have the PSI report—I imagined being at Santa Rosa for weeks. At about seven that evening, the night commander sent for me. He asked me when I last ate, and I said, "Around seven this morning." He offered to have the kitchen fix me something, which I appreciated. He asked me how long I was going to be there and what crime I committed.

"I didn't commit any crime," I said, "but you probably hear that all the time. I'm here for six months."

He assured me the time would pass quickly as long as I read the rulebook and followed supervisors' orders. He said I could call Candy once I arrived at Santa Rosa, but it was against the rules to inform anyone prior to a transport. I was served a tray of spaghetti and bread, but even after nearly twelve hours, I didn't have much of an appetite.

The reality of prison life set in when guards put me in handcuffs and leg irons for the ride to Santa Rosa. The chains got caught in a hole as I tried to navigate stairs, cutting my leg. The van had bars on the doors and windows. We traveled on a causeway with water on both sides, and my state of mind had me imagining what would happen if the vehicle flipped—I wouldn't stand a chance of getting out of the van under water and surviving. I felt a little relief when the officer driving told me I'd be separated from the general population at the jail and housed with other federal prisoners. Upon arrival, I was processed again along with about ten others, issued different prison attire, and finally allowed to call Candy.

I was told my time at Santa Rosa would be credited toward my sentence. That was about the only good news I had for the night, and I couldn't bear to hear the distress in Candy's voice.

Carrying my issued bedroll and pillow, I felt like I was in an old James Cagney prison movie. To my surprise, the cellblock was overflowing with inmates, not seven or eight as I'd been told. There was no way to navigate through the aisle to my cell, so using the bedroll as a battering ram, I lowered my head and pushed through the crowd. I actually expected fists to fly, but I was so angry it didn't matter.

My cellmate introduced himself and said he was also a federal prisoner. "Which bunk do you want?" he asked.

I could see he'd already taken the lower bunk, but probably noticing my age, graciously offered to switch.

"The top is fine," I said. To be honest, I figured it was easier to punch down than up. "How long have you been here?" I asked.

"Fifteen months now."

"You must be kidding!" Was Santa Rosa Jail going to be my home for the duration of my sentence? My cellmate kindly offered a snack from his accumulation of commissary items over the last fifteen months, but I declined. I was physically and mentally drained, and simply looking forward to a good night's sleep. He must have been amused, because as soon as the lights went out, the screaming and singing began. My bunkie told me the guys sleep during the day, played cards or worked out in the evening, and then stayed up all night making noise. I was in jail.

At about four o'clock in the morning, a voice on the loudspeaker summoned me to the cellblock entrance. The jail nurse told me my blood pressure was very high when I arrived the night before, and gave me medication. Then an officer offered breakfast since I was already up.

"Why not, what's on the menu?" I answered. It was scrambled eggs, coffee, toast, and juice.

"I'm a customer," I thought. When he brought the food, I didn't see the eggs until I tilted the tray and figured the runny mess was supposed to be the main course. I also opted for water after tasting the coffee and juice...it was going to be a long stay. I didn't bring my Bible and glasses because the officer at Eglin warned they'd probably get lost. The only sources of sanity were going to be the telephone and some religious publications my roommate had. At least I lucked out with him. During the next couple days, it was obvious he was well respected among the inmates, and at only about 175 pounds, was a workout guru and very strong. We got along well for the short time we were together. I just couldn't believe he'd been there for fifteen months.

"The county loves federal prisoners," he explained. "The feds pay sixty-seven dollars a day to house and feed us."

How many federal prisons would it take to get inmates out of county jails? Prior to becoming number 57918-066, I was very conservative when it came to white-collar crime. "Throw the book at them," I always thought. But my perspective changed. What is the rationale behind sending first-time, non-violent offenders to prison for extended periods? One young man was nineteen-years-old when he received a fourteen-year sentence for selling drugs. This is one reason the prison population has grown at an alarming rate, and Congress needs to address this issue. The 85 percent rule, whereby all federal offenders must serve at least 85 percent of their sentence, isn't working. My observations have nothing to do with my case, but point to a flawed, out-of-control system that is unnecessarily costing taxpayers.

On Wednesday morning my cellmate was fairly certain he was finally getting transferred to a federal prison to serve the rest of his four-year sentence. He offered me several items, but I just asked for his copy of *The Upper Room*. He also said I should switch to the lower bunk, but I told him I liked the view. Within a few hours, he was gone, and I was genuinely happy for him.

I knew I had to try and sleep during the day, so I tried to relax by reading the pamphlet. The words instantly had a calming effect—*trust in the Lord...all things happen in His time...be patient*. There was the key word again: *patience*. I would need it during the next six months and for a long time after my release. As I continued reading, I started drifting off, but fortunately I wasn't dreaming when a voice over the loudspeaker woke me. "Scott Brown, report to the front, you are being moved to Eglin." I was ready within minutes. The process that started three days earlier was finally going to be finished.

This time there were no shackles. I was reprocessed at Eglin on Wednesday, January 14, 2004, got my Bible and reading glasses, and was assigned to a top corner bunk in Dorm B. The units were divided into four sections, each with twenty-four cubicles. Several inmates introduced themselves and helped me get settled, including demonstrating the proper way to make the bunk. I was exhausted, but I had arrived after dinner, so I was also starving. My stomach had been quite upset the previous day and I'd only consumed maybe a handful of food since Monday. I was thankful when the inmate in the next cubicle said, "Sonny, you look like you can use an orange." I wolfed it down and he offered me an apple, which I also gladly accepted. His name was Charlie Elliott, and he then offered to buy me ice cream from the prison canteen. I didn't have a commissary card yet, so I'll always remember Charlie's kindness that night.

I was allowed to call Candy to let her know I was back at Eglin

"Good. Now make sure they have my name on the visitors' list. I'm coming this weekend."

"No, Candy. I don't want you to come here at all." I had put my family through enough. I didn't want them to see me in prison, plus Eglin was a seven-hour drive from Orlando—it was nerve-wracking to think of her on the road that long for a two-way trip over a couple days.

"Scott, I'm coming, you can't keep me away, so you better make the proper arrangements."

We debated this point, and a prison counselor even talked to Candy about respecting my wishes, but she was adamant. We finally agreed she'd visit one day, and if I didn't want her to return, she would concede. I genuinely wanted to spare my family any more heartache, but I simply didn't realize that visiting helped her healing process. Seeing me finish the horrid ordeal was part of its closure.

Candy's darkest day was shortly after I arrived at Eglin. The doorbell rang and the postman had a package. He even apologized and said it was probably a mistake because he could see the box was from the prison.

"I opened it and there were the clothes you had on when you left," she said. "It was so impersonal, and it seemed like you were a million miles away instead of a couple hundred. I felt completely helpless and it just brought me to my knees."

Accompanied by my daughter, Meredith, Candy came to Eglin that first weekend and nearly every one after.

From my perspective, I just wanted to plow ahead and finish my sentence. The first two weeks were an indoctrination period at the prison, and I met my supervisor, Officer Merriweather, an African-American and the sharpest dressed staff member I met during my six months. He turned out to be tough but fair, returning the respect he demanded of the inmates. Raking leaves for the first two weeks at Eglin was tradition, and during that time, Merriweather had good advice: do your time honorably and return to your loved ones who depend on you. That was my obligation. He said he wasn't dumb enough to believe everyone at Eglin was guilty of the crimes that landed them in prison.

Merriweather also kept us laughing, and the weeks passed quickly. He shared stories about his family, especially his son and ongoing battles to have the trash bagged and discarded in a precise manner. I believe he genuinely cared about the inmates and was noticeably concerned when someone was ill or not getting necessary medical attention.

When it was time to report for a permanent assignment, I was designated to be an aide to the Warden instead of a grounds-keeping job, but the warden's secretary learned I was only sentenced to six months, and she didn't want to retrain somebody that quickly, so I was assigned to maintaining a five-acre tract of land, once again reporting to officer Merriweather. It was a blessing; I love the outdoors, and my other supervisor, Officer Ramsey, was a straight shooter who just expected the work to be done.

A normal day at Eglin started about 5:30 a.m. with breakfast, and then a half hour in the prison chapel before reporting to my assigned job. At ten o'clock in the morning, I would head to lunch with two inmates, Frankie and Roy. The three of us shared a lot of laughter in an otherwise gloomy situation. The days ended with a call home, and even though we didn't have to be in our bunks until ten, I was usually asleep by nine. Naturally I was not happy to be punished for a crime I didn't commit, but I was making the best of a bad situation and grateful to be at a prison camp instead of a medium security facility. Of course there were unpleasant inmates, and a few guards were referred to as "crazies," but, overall, people were fair and decent.

During my incarceration, I read the Bible from cover to cover, and several other books that nurtured my walk with the Lord, including *The Case for Christ* by Lee Strobel. This was given to me by Father Bob Montford, assistant rector at my church in Lake Mary, Florida. It was one of his favorite books, and it was a great blessing to me during a difficult time.

I often describe my prison experience as my "come to Jesus meeting." For the first time in my life, God had my undivided attention and I was totally committed to learning all I could. There were no business meetings, no urgent phone calls, and no places to go or people to see—it was just Jesus and me. I believe He planned it that way and it was His perfect timing. I attended a Bible study or church service nearly every evening after dinner.

During the thirty-four years prior to incarceration, I seldom missed a Sunday church service. What I had previously learned about God was through Sunday school classes as a young boy and then what I heard from the pulpit as an adult. I occasionally read the Bible, usually motivated by something I'd heard or witnessed that would pique my curiosity. There in prison, though, after the struggle I'd been through, I was at a different place in my life, and my desire to study God's Word was intense.

As I began my daily walk with the Lord, reading the Bible literally consumed me. When I wasn't reading the Bible, you could find me at a Bible study or a worship service in the prison chapel. The more I read and studied, the easier my incarceration became. Reading the Bible was an exciting experience for me. I could hardly put it down, and when I did, I couldn't wait to pick it up again because God was revealing Himself to me through His holy and inspired Word. It also brought new light to Christian-related books that also nurtured me—a whole new world opened up for me. What God did in my life was more than I deserved.

I never had a bad day at Eglin Federal Prison Camp. I attribute this to the fact that I was walking with God and this walk was, in fact, His walk. Despite the scars the prior three years left on me, I experienced serenity and laughter on a daily basis. Even to this day, it never ceases to amaze me that God found me in a place that I never thought I would be, but now I understand God will never take you where His grace is not sufficient to sustain you.

God is good...all the time, and He soon revealed more of His perfect timing and incredible plan for my life.

Chapter 11
UNLIKELY COMPANY

W HAT I DIDN'T EXPECT AT EGLIN WAS THE EXTRAORDINARY circumstance that manifested about two weeks after I arrived. I was asleep in my bunk when someone shined a flashlight in my face.

"Are you Scott Brown?" It was a prison counselor. "I have a new inmate here who is asking to see you."

I tried to adjust my eyes. "I don't know anyone coming here."

"He said he used to work for Morgan Crucible and specifically asked for you. I'd appreciate it if you could help me get him settled."

The counselor turned the flashlight on the inmate.

"This is Robin Emerson."

> In his heart a man plans his course, but the LORD determines his steps.
>
> —PROVERBS 16:9

I'd only met Emerson once, at the infamous meeting in Toronto in 1997. Now seven years later he stood next to my prison bunk, disheveled and ashen. He'd also spent some unpleasant days and nights at Santa Rosa County Jail. I helped him as much as possible that evening before the ten o'clock bed check, showing him how to prepare his cubicle and bunk space, putting away his belongings, and then became his guide around the prison the next day.

Over the next few months, Emerson, a British citizen, revealed incredible information about Morgan Crucible's practices as part of a European cartel, as well as details that supported my innocence. I knew very little about him prior to this. My first attorney, Chan Muller, tried to interview him, but Emerson refused. Now, having landed in prison, he was ready to talk. I asked him why he requested Eglin. He said it was due to my reputation, which at the time seemed an incongruous remark—I'd only met Emerson once, at that Toronto meeting. I had no opinion of him, other than wondering what his place was within Morgan Crucible. As time went on and he explained his role, it became clear he knew a lot about my actions and about me.

This was certainly divine intervention! It was too late to save me from prison, but I knew better than to question God's timing.

Emerson was a longtime colleague of Ian Norris, and he was the "score-keeper" for Morgan Crucible's activities in the cartel, claiming to have recorded notes in his diary from 144 price-fixing meetings. He wasn't highly paid, roughly forty-five thousand dollars a year, but obviously enjoyed his friendship with Norris and notoriety from his cartel activities.

Emerson entered his plea agreement with the Justice Department on December 6, 2003, which originally stipulated a six-month period of confinement, but was amended to five months because Emerson was neither an officer nor director of Morgan Crucible or one of its subsidiaries. He went on to say he was interviewed the day after his plea hearing by AUSA McClain and members of her staff at the Department of Justice Antitrust Division in Philadelphia and was asked the following questions:

The Justice Department staff showed Emerson a handwritten document and asked him if he recognized the author's handwriting. He said he didn't. *(Emerson told me it belonged to Ian Norris.)*

Was the meeting held on January 29, 1997, in Toronto, a price-fixing meeting? Yes, Emerson said.

Was F. Scott Brown at the Toronto meeting? Yes, Emerson said.

What he didn't tell them was that Joseph Klatt from Schunk made outrageous demands and I blew up and left before the meeting ended. "They didn't ask those questions," Emerson said.

This was alarming. I had provided written and verbal commentary about what happened in Toronto to my attorney, Joe Tate, and I assumed he shared this information with AUSA Rosenberg in response to statements made by Joe Klatt, Tony Massaro, and Jim Floyd. The Justice Department prosecutors must have had my account of the Toronto meeting, yet they didn't ask Emerson any related questions, for example: did Joe Klatt propose splitting the John Crane resin bonded business?

Did Klatt threaten to acquire Metalized Carbon in order to make things difficult for Morgan AM&T? Did I tell Klatt that Schunk would have to earn every penny of business it received in the United States? Did I leave the meeting, and what happened afterward? I could think of a dozen unasked questions, but apparently the DOJ wasn't interested in verifying anything I said. Again, so much for getting to the truth.

Emerson had a lot more to share:

After Morgan Crucible received the 1999 subpoena, Bill Macfarlane, chairman of the Carbon Division, and Mel Perkins, sales manager at Morgan Crucible's Electrical Carbon, Ltd., repeatedly encouraged Emerson not to cooperate with the Justice Department (he said he had diary entries of at least seven meetings about this issue).

Emerson said he'd simply followed instructions from Bill Macfarlane and Mel Perkins not to cooperate with Justice Department officials, and his only chance of avoiding prison was for Norris, CEO of Morgan Crucible, to come clean. At one point, the DOJ offered Norris a four-year sentence and Emerson's attorney intervened with the DOJ and had it reduced to one year if Norris would cooperate. Norris refused, believing he could get the sentence down to eight months. Emerson believed his chance at any deal to stay out of prison evaporated at that point.

Morgan Crucible also did to Emerson what it had done to me—cancelled his indemnification for "unreasonable" legal fees (a trial)—in other words, fall on your sword, or we won't pay.

Jack Kroef, formerly global president of Morgan Crucible's Industrial & Rail Traction business, was serving a four-month sentence at the Pensacola Federal Prison Camp for witness tampering. Emerson said Kroef was a major player in the cartel scheme in the United States and Europe.

At a Carbon Executive Review meeting in Windsor in early 2000, Jack Kroef, while passing me in the hallway, stated, "Schunk hates your guts." I thought, "What a strange thing to say," and where did the comment originate? Why did someone say that to Kroef? I smiled and replied, "You just made my day."

During my career with Morgan Crucible there is only one occasion when Kroef and I had any business discussions. I had sent Simon Hussey to France to look at a Morgan Crucible operation that was supposedly

50 percent electrical and 50 percent mechanical carbon. Upon Hussey's return, he recommended closing the facility and moving the mechanical equipment where it could be used, which made Kroef very angry, and he sent a memo to Ian Norris that was highly critical of Hussey's decision. At the time, I believe Kroef's attitude had something to do with the cartel arrangements between Morgan and Carbone. I guess you might say my actions were affecting the cartel in several areas and causing aggravation that I was not aware of or fully comprehended.

Jack Kroef was highly intelligent, but in the last years of his employment at Morgan Crucible, he consistently failed to produce the results he had forecast. I could sense there was deterioration in the relationship Kroef once enjoyed with Ian Norris. This was most evident at the global presidents' quarterly presentations and reviews.

My revealing discussions with Robin Emerson continued:

When I told Emerson that Edye Thein, former sales manager for Morgan AM&T–Europe, received a $1.8 million payment in addition to his normal retirement package, Emerson seemed shocked and said he'd only been given $270,000 to stonewall the DOJ, but was made to appear as part of a severance package, and to legitimize the move, Morgan Crucible had Emerson sign an agreement not to work for competitors.

Emerson was very bitter over how he'd been hung out to dry. Several executives were heavily involved in cartel activities on the electrical side in the United States, and Emerson believed that they, along with several European executives should have all been sent to prison. I provided the Justice Department with the list of those named by Emerson.

He then went on to tell me he had no idea why I, of all people, was in prison. He acknowledged that I had had nothing to do with price fixing. His knowledge of my innocence was music to my ears, but things really boiled over when we spent several hours over the course of a few days talking about various meetings—clearly the ones referenced by the DOJ when they revealed accusations made by Klatt, Floyd, and Massaro to my attorneys:[1]

First, I was shocked to hear that Massaro had been working with Norris and Bryce for quite a while before the Toronto meeting, and regularly communicated with Emerson. Massaro had told Jim Younger that he didn't know Emerson, except maybe a brief encounter while visiting the Morriston plant in the United Kingdom where Emerson worked.

Emerson revealed that he met with Massaro in December 1996 or early January 1997, a month before the Toronto meeting, at The Castle Hotel in Windsor, United Kingdom, to set prices for John Crane. I came back to the topic a few times to make absolutely sure I understood him. He described this meeting as a difficult undertaking because of the number of parts involved and exchange rates in different countries where John Crane conducted business.

These comments speak to information that AUSA Rosenberg shared with Chris Levine, an attorney in Tate's firm, in January 2003. Levine couldn't make complete sense of the notes, other than the information was related to Schunk and Morgan Crucible's pricing for John Crane and some sort of difficulty as a result of U.S./European pricing differential. I believe those notes refer to the meeting between Massaro and Emerson at the Castle Hotel. The fact that the meeting ever took place is proof Massaro was working with other members of the cartel before the Toronto meeting.

Even before this, in November or early December 1996, Emerson had met with Norris, Thein, and Bryce from Morgan Crucible and representatives from Schunk, including Joseph Klatt and Dr. Bruckmann, at Frederick's Resort Restaurant in Maidenhead for a discussion about the Flexibox and John Crane accounts. Emerson said Klatt pushed Morgan for cooperation on setting prices. That's when the Toronto meeting was first discussed. Emerson was picked to represent Morgan Crucible because of my dealings with Bryce and Thein, and because I didn't know Emerson.

Emerson also confirmed the sequence of events at the Toronto meeting. While I was still present, Klatt made demands about getting 50 percent of the John Crane resin bonded business or else Schunk would buy Metalized Carbon Company and make things tough for Morgan AM&T. Klatt also said Morgan AM&T–Europe had 30 percent of the business there, and Schunk wanted 30 percent in the United States. The meeting then turned into a shouting match, and after twenty minutes I left the room. Emerson said he took over after I left, and for forty-five minutes to an hour, Klatt and Massaro exchanged documents and agreed on pricing for John Crane.

Massaro later faxed Emerson a seventeen-page document that listed eight hundred John Crane parts and was set up with three separate columns: one had the Morgan AM&T prices, one had Schunk's prices, and there was a third column for remarks. Massaro had told me and investigator Jim Younger that he thought John Crane gave our prices to Schunk—now obviously a lie.

In one of my meetings with my attorney, Joe Tate, I learned Massaro was going to testify that I instructed him to prepare a seventeen-page document listing some eight hundred John Crane part numbers, quantities, and prices. According to Massaro, I told him to bring it to the Toronto meeting. This was a lie.

Massaro would also testify that he didn't have time to prepare the document before the Toronto meeting. Lie number two.

Morgan AM&T had already quoted all of John Crane's requirements—roughly one thousand parts—and submitted the quotes to Crane's offices at Mortin Grove. These prices were on Massaro's computer. Massaro told private investigator Jim Younger he thought John Crane gave our prices to Schunk. Lie number three. When his lies caught up with him, Massaro said I instructed him to prepare the Crane parts list after the Toronto meeting and send it to Robin Emerson. Lie number four.

This is the same Tony Massaro who met secretly with Emerson one month before the Toronto meeting and then told me he may have met Emerson once while visiting the Morriston plant. Lie number five.

The dictionary defines *perjurer* as "one who tells lies: fabricator, fabulist, falsifier, fibster, liar, and prevaricator."[2] I don't know if Massaro, Floyd, or Klatt actually testified before the grand jury, but I know they didn't tell the truth, the whole truth, and nothing but the truth.

> The LORD detests lying lips, but he delights in men who are truthful.
> —PROVERBS 12:22

Schunk's prices for John Crane were on the documents Massaro sent Emerson because Massaro entered them in the column next to our pricing after exchanging documents with Klatt at the Toronto meeting. Unfortunately for me, Klatt, Floyd, and Massaro had very convenient memories of what took place in Toronto on January 29, 1997.

Of course, it all made sense now. That's how Massaro got Schunk's prices—it didn't make sense that I was the one sitting in prison. I never knew this information until Emerson told me during our shared prison experience.

I thought back to Massaro's early statement to my attorney's investigator, Jim Younger, about how I got upset in Toronto and had the "old Pure Carbon" attitude. Massaro was entrenched in the cartel loop at that point, and must have hoped I'd go along. Emerson said he had several telephone conversations with Massaro, both prior to and after the Toronto meeting, centered around John Crane business for the most part, but also about other customers. He said Massaro always had to have the last word; "He was the expert." Emerson clearly didn't like him. I'd known Massaro for nearly thirty years—he and I worked together on my first major sales success—and the depth of betrayal in his follow-up testimony to the Department of Justice was appalling and dishonest. He failed to tell the whole story for obvious reasons.

Emerson's next shocking piece of information was that I was the subject of a second meeting in Toronto the following day between him, Joe Klatt, and Jim Floyd from Schunk, when Klatt complained to Emerson that I was putting pressure on Schunk's business and wanted Ian Norris to intervene and get me to back off. Emerson reported the matter to Bryce, but I never heard anything about the matter. Klatt was right about at least that much—I had applied intense pressure on all Schunk's business in the United States, and when I became global president, I did the same thing in Europe, particularly in Germany.

I then mentioned to Emerson the claims Klatt made about another meeting, "He told the DOJ that when I met him in Giessen, Germany, it was agreed that he, you, and I would set prices in Europe."

Emerson said it was news to him, and described it all as pure garbage.

Klatt also told the Justice Department that he and I openly discussed pricing for John Crane, Gast Manufacturing, Procon Products, Chicago Allis, A.W. Chesterton, and Franklin Electric. A cursory review of my files for these accounts would have proven this was a total fabrication.

Emerson said I was released from my European responsibilities because of Bryce's termination, and Ian Norris was convinced I'd never cooperate with the cartel. I scared the hell out of the German cartel members when I opened the low-cost manufacturing facility in Hungary and added additional salespeople and application engineers to go after Schunk and SGL's business in Germany.

Emerson also said Norris was constantly settling disputes because there was considerable distrust between Thein, Bryce, and Klatt. It wasn't surprising to me. When an operation is based on secrets and cover-ups, people are going to constantly look over their shoulders for the slip that brings it crashing down. In fact, the central dilemma of a cartel is that it carries its own seeds of destruction. In order to dominate a market, members have to agree and fully cooperate on how to dictate price, control supply, and keep the whole scheme in the shadows. A cartel works well in an industry like carbon manufacturing because there are high barriers to market entry and few big customers, making it easier to hold everything together. Players trade bigger profits for long-term stability, but any single member can defect for a quick gain and then destabilize the entire framework. I was clearly a threat (although I didn't even know it), especially after dismissing Bryce and redirecting Morgan AM&T-Europe's focus toward customer service, sustained growth, and cost reductions, all aimed at obtaining new business. I upset the apple cart far too much—quite contrary to AUSA McClain's assessment that I went along to get along.

I asked Emerson why Norris didn't just drop out of the cartel when Morgan Crucible acquired Pure Carbon, the powerhouse in the United States. It didn't make sense; Morgan Crucible didn't need to take the risk. Emerson said Klatt insisted that mechanical carbon be in the mix, especially because Schunk only had 1 percent of the U.S. mechanical carbon market. Norris reluctantly agreed because Morgan Crucible was weak on the electrical side and needed cooperation from Schunk and Carbone.

According to Emerson, the electrical cartel in North America began in Canada between Carbone representatives and executives from Morganite, Inc. and National Electrical Carbon. All these executives received immunity from prosecution from the U.S. government. Emerson said there were four more meetings between the two companies directly related to the auto consumer carbon brush business in the United States. The Morganite executives were aware of all pricing arrangements, and Emerson believes they threatened to blow the whistle on Ian Norris if Morgan Crucible didn't protect them during the Justice Department investigation.

I first met the Morganite executive while attending a National Electrical Manufacturer's Association (NEMA) conference. He was the president of Morganite at the time, and I was president of the Pure Carbon Company. Under this executive, Morganite consisted of a large consumer automotive brush business and a small mechanical carbon unit located in Dunn, North Carolina.

When Morgan Crucible acquired Pure Carbon Company in March 1995, the Morganite executive was most helpful to me by providing insight into the company's protocol and suggestions relative to what management expected in both the form and length of business presentations. We often sat together at the quarterly general managers' meetings as well as the annual meetings.

In my opinion, this individual was one of the best managers in the Morgan Crucible group of companies. Despite this assessment, I was surprised when he was chosen to be the global president of the Technical Ceramics business in 1998, reporting to Nigel Howard. This business was totally foreign to him and he experienced numerous personnel and business issues, which he shared with me from time to time.

Shortly after I was served my subpoena, David Coker called to tell me that Morgan Crucible had turned over thousands of price-fixing documents to the European Commission. He also told me that the pricing documents had been stored in a garage near Jack Kroef's residence in Horne, Holland. He said he wasn't at liberty to divulge the source of this information, but he was confident the disclosure would personally benefit me. I thanked him for the information. Interestingly, the calls from Coker stopped when Morgan cut their deal with the DOJ.

Emerson said Ian Norris and Kroef met with the Germans (Klatt and someone else whose name Emerson couldn't recall) at the Heathrow Airport in an attempt to persuade the Germans to stonewall the Justice Department. This was interesting because Klatt told the DOJ that he and I had four meetings and the last one was at the Heathrow Airport and included Laurence Bryce. This was totally false and misleading.

Reading my indictment and the indictments of Emerson, Kroef, and

Norris, I was appalled to see that Edye Thein, Laurence Bryce, and Mel Perkins would appear as witnesses for the prosecution if I went to trial. How could this ever happen? These were people heavily involved in cartel activities spanning many years. At this point, the conspiracy was obviously continuing and I can only assume to know who was behind the agreement to have these individuals testify against me. Who brokered this deal?

I couldn't believe that by placing Emerson in prison with me, God handed me so many pieces to the insane, frustrating puzzle I'd been trying to put together for three years. So much of what happened hadn't made sense—now it all came together.

On Friday, January 30, 2004, Dave Quinn and his wife, Jeanne, came to see me at the prison camp during regular visitor's hours. During my conversation with them, I remarked that Robin Emerson and his wife, Yvonne, were also in the visitor's room. I told Dave that I was going to introduce him to Emerson and then excuse myself to go to the bathroom, hoping that Emerson would tell Dave what he'd told me. While I was out of the room, Emerson and Quinn engaged in a conversation that covered many of the issues I'd discussed with Emerson. Quinn later told me Emerson said, "Scott is an innocent man. He had nothing to do with price fixing." Quinn said he felt Emerson was very remorseful, and that's why he shared information with us.

Early in February 2004, Emerson had disturbing news: according to his attorney, he and I were going to be subpoenaed to testify in a civil lawsuit brought against Morgan Crucible by electrical customers. I couldn't believe it—I was already serving time for something I didn't do, and I had never sold one product to the plaintiffs in the suit—where was the justice? How much did I have to endure?

I was eventually moved to another dorm and didn't have regular daily contact with Emerson. I'm forever thankful for God's grace putting us together. There are numerous federal prisons in the United States—what are the chances that the one person who had not testified against me somehow ended up at Eglin at the same time? This was not chance. God clearly wanted to lift a heavy burden from Emerson's heart and also provide me with key facts to help clarify the course of events that led to my prison sentence. God turned the darkness into light. Emerson thanked me for my friendship in a letter after he was released:[3]

> "Anyway Scott, the real purpose of this letter is to express my profound thanks to you for your friendship....I hope that in a small way, I was able to reciprocate and in talking through our respective situations, perhaps help you come to terms with the injustice that had fallen upon you, and the anger that you still felt about the way you had been treated by the company."

As upset as I was about my situation, my heart was sad for him. Yes, he participated in price fixing on behalf of Morgan Crucible, but, in my opinion, he was a pawn when the cartel was exposed in the United States and shouldn't have been prosecuted. It's inconceivable that certain senior officials and members of the board of directors and the executive committee of Morgan Crucible were never prosecuted, while a low-salaried employee who followed their orders went to prison. The fact that he wasn't an officer or director in the company shaved only one month off his six-month sentence.

AUSA McClain's Canadian counterpart tried to warn Emerson that Morgan Crucible was attempting to blame him for the price-fixing activities that had occurred in Canada. Emerson was too trusting to understand the lengths certain people would go to protect the Morgan Crucible hierarchy.

During his stay at Eglin, Emerson continually worried that Morgan Crucible would cut off his financial support, which included living expenses for his family and their travel costs to visit him at Eglin. (I had Candy contact Morgan Crucible about reimbursing us, and it came through, perhaps because I was going to testify in the civil case.) Emerson also feared the Canadian government would come after him as soon as he was released from Eglin, but Morgan Crucible's attorneys brokered immunity for him, and he returned to his family in England. Morgan Crucible paid one million dollars Canadian for violations in Canada. "A very low fine," Emerson wrote, "but at whose expense?"

Chapter 12

TRUE FREEDOM

MERSON'S REVELATIONS BOLSTERED MY DETERMINATION TO pursue a modicum of justice. I talked to another inmate who was a former attorney, and he said it might be possible to file a Racketeer Influenced and Corrupt Organizations (RICO) treble damages lawsuit because it appeared Morgan Crucible's management acted in bad faith and conspired against me by taking away my indemnification and making false or misleading statements about a memo I wrote summarizing my meetings with Schunk. Bill Macfarlane told me Ian Norris requested the summary. Morgan Crucible apparently turned my memo over to the Justice Department and portrayed them as price-fixing meetings with the "competition." It was tempting—defendants in RICO cases risk public branding as racketeers, and if they lose, pay out triple damages, punitive damages, and litigation costs and fees.

The first step toward any resolution was getting the transcript from my court hearing, and I asked Candy to begin the process. My friend, Steve Salley, also an attorney, advised me to wait until I left prison before contacting the Justice Department about any further action in my case. Looking back, when it became clear the government was going after me, Salley said if he were in my shoes, he'd ask for a plea agreement on day one, sign on the dotted line, and get it over with as quickly as possible. He knew what I was in for; going against the U.S. government was futile, and Morgan Crucible had deep pockets to protect itself above all else. My ignorance wasn't bliss.

Looking through the transcript from my court appearance, I more fully realized I was into a catch-22—if I responded honestly and completely, Judge Brody would have thrown out the plea and slated my case for trial. Morgan Crucible had withdrawn my indemnification, and if I went to trial, I would have been totally on my own financially. I'd been advised that the cost could have run as high as three million dollars, which included a one million-dollar fine, and the Justice Department would have ramped up the charges against me to include price fixing, meaning I could have spent forty months in prison if I lost. Quite honestly, I could have handled that term because I believe a trial would have exposed both Schunk and Morgan Crucible's involvement, but I wasn't prepared to bankrupt my family and put my wife and ninety-one-year-old mother-in-law on the street. This was my dilemma!

In the end, I found Judge Brody to be fair and impartial. Her job was to assure that I accepted the content of the plea, but I was backed into a corner. I'm sure this situation wasn't new to her, but somehow I feel I failed her attempt to uphold justice that day.

Before I left Eglin, I had to deal with the civil lawsuit filed by electrical customers against Morganite and Morgan Crucible. It named me, Robin Emerson, Ian Norris, and Jack Kroef as defendants, even though I was never involved in the electrical side of the business. Joe Tate represented me, and Morgan Crucible paid my legal fees. It was disturbing that they would cover my expenses in a civil suit, but not the criminal case. It was all about avoiding negative publicity and controlling monetary damages, but for me it was about integrity and justice. In the end, Tate successfully had my name removed from the suit, and Morgan Crucible negotiated a settlement with the plaintiffs.

I spent the last night at Eglin eating nachos with men I'd come to know and care about, and then headed to chapel one last time to thank God for sharing my burden and providing me with the determination and revelations to clear my name. I gave thanks for my wonderful wife, family, friends, and colleagues. I received more than seven hundred letters of support during my incarceration!

Candy and my children anxiously planned a wonderful gathering for my welcome home party, preparing ham, potato salad, and baked beans at my request. I woke at five o'clock on July 9, 2004, and packed. I gave away food and clothing to some fellow inmates, including athletic shoes, a prized possession for those who couldn't afford them. Someone hung a sign reading "Elvis has left the building" in honor of my rendition of "Heartbreak Hotel" at a few musical shows at Eglin, and I smiled at the small tribute. As I walked down the corridor for the last time, I knew I was a better man because my Lord and Savior walked with me throughout the entire journey.

My son, Rick, and son-in-law, Greg, picked me up. They had the unpleasant task of dropping me off at the airport when I left for prison, so I wanted them to bring me home. A prison officer drove me a couple miles to a remote parking area, and there they were. I was free to get out of the prison van, hug them, and go home. "You're not driving today, dad," Rick said. I laughed, and cried.

I know it was "only" six months, but I was filled with wonder and exuberance looking out the car window at God's creation—trees, the sky, birds. I thought about freedom, and about people like Senator John McCain, who endured six years and excruciating conditions as a prisoner of war in Vietnam. My experience paled in comparison, but never again will I take my freedom for granted.

"There are a few people who'd like to hear from you," Greg said. "Some of your friends at Morgan AM&T in St. Marys are waiting for a phone call."

When I announced, "I'm out," there was a roar at the other end of the line. These personal and professional friends supported my family and me throughout our ordeal. We also had the camaraderie of knowing that Pure Carbon Company and later Morgan AM&T never became part of the cartel, even though some individuals were involved in the wrongdoing and possibly were the same individuals who met in Mexico City to allocate market share and set prices for mechanical carbon products sold in the U.S. Later, Morgan AM&T and Scott Brown were named in civil lawsuits brought by Morganite Electrical's customer. Why? I'll never know. But in any event, it was an emotional telephone call for me.

Arriving home, Candy was at the door and we held on to each other and shared our tears. I was overcome by the love of my family and friends. My children made the seven-hour trip with Candy to Eglin on a regular basis; Candy's brothers took over caring for her mom during this time; Rev. David Vaughn, Dave Quinn, and others wrote me every week. Now we all celebrated my homecoming. The Lord blessed me richly—my cup runneth over, even in the darkest depths of the valley.

The next day I caught up with a neighbor and went to the golf club to say hello to a couple of friends, and then Candy and I prepared to go to the beach for a month. She had made arrangements, just wanting the whole family to relax. Joe Tate called while we were there to wish me well.

"Scott, you were [railroaded]," he said, but in slightly more descriptive terminology, and repeated the statement a few times during our conversation, but never elaborated as to why he was so convinced. Maybe he learned more details while I was in prison.

We decompressed during our stay at the beach. My children and grandchildren visited often, and Candy and I tried to focus on the future. I realized that the six months were extraordinarily difficult for her, while I found it nearly a relief after fighting so hard for almost three years.

"I focused on deepening my journey with God," I told her, "so that's what the days were about, and He carried me through. And who could have imagined He'd give me the chance to talk about what happened with Robin Emerson!"

Candy knew I was hinting at more action on my case, and that wasn't what she wanted to hear. "All those sleepless nights, I couldn't take away the hurt you were going through, as much as I prayed for it to stop," she said. "I just want it to end now, but I'll support whatever you feel you need to do."

In August 2004, following our family vacation at the beach, several of our friends and former colleagues held a welcome home party for Candy and me in St. Marys, Pennsylvania. The event's organizers attempted to reserve the Pure Carbon Lodge for the occasion, but when word reached Morgan Crucible's new management team in Greenville, South Carolina, my friends were told the party couldn't take place at the lodge. The venue was moved to the St. Marys Country Club where several hundred folks took time from their busy schedules to remember and visit with the Browns. It was a wonderful opportunity for Candy and me to thank so many for their notes of encouragement, unwavering support, and especially their faithful prayers, which covered us during some very difficult and tumultuous events. We will treasure that day in our hearts forever.

The following Sunday, I was invited to address the congregation at the United Methodist Church, which our family had previously attended. I humbly accepted Pastor Vaughn's invitation, and my testimony that day centered on the trials and tribulations of the Apostle Paul and what it meant to become a soldier for our Lord Jesus Christ. Those in attendance that Sunday may have expected to hear about my incarceration or criminal case, but I thought those subjects would be inappropriate; after all, this was God's house and I went there on a mission to glorify His holy name. There weren't many dry eyes in the church at the end of service, including mine and Pastor Vaughn's. We serve a great God.

The first order of business after our retreat and trip to St. Marys was orthopedic surgery on my arthritic knees. During my recovery, I explored filing the RICO lawsuit against Morgan Crucible, but learned it would be difficult because of my plea agreement, and the case would have to be tried in Pennsylvania, not Florida. It's very costly litigation and it would have been a challenge to find an attorney willing to take it on a contingency basis.

About that time, I received a letter from the prestigious London law firm White and Case, attorneys for Ian Norris, noting the following:

> Mr. Norris was indicted in the United States in October 2003 on charges of price fixing and obstruction of justice. We enclose a copy of the current indictment, which is the second superseding indictment filed on 28 September 2004 ("the indictment"). The essence of the price fixing charges is that from before 1989 Mr. Norris participated on behalf of Morgan in a worldwide cartel of carbon products, which extended in 1989 to the United States and continued for more than a decade until 2000. The essence of the obstruction of justice charges is that Mr. Norris took steps from 1999 onwards to impede the Department of Justice's investigation into the alleged cartel. The charges will be vigorously defended.
>
> The United States government has issued a request to the government of Great Britain for the extradition of Mr. Norris to stand trial. The extradition hearing is due to take place on 10–12 May 2005 and will be strongly contested.
>
> We believe you have knowledge relevant to Mr. Norris' defense. In your position as global President at Morgan, your knowledge of the relationship between Morgan and its competitors, the operation of the alleged cartel, and Mr. Norris' involvement in the operation

of the alleged cartel during the 1980s and 1990s is highly relevant to Mr. Norris' defense of the charges.

In the first instance, please let us know the following:

Do you generally recall these matters?

Would you, in principle, be prepared to give evidence on behalf of Mr. Norris at a trial in the United States if he is extradited?

Are you prepared to give evidence, if necessary, at the extradition hearing in London in May, either in person or by affidavit?

Do you possess, or have you previously possessed, any documents relevant to the issues that appear to arise in the Indictment?

We would appreciate your response to this letter, if possible by 1 April 2005.

My attorney, Joe Tate, also received a copy of the letter, and we agreed to respond that I had no interest getting involved in Norris's case. I never concocted any statements to implicate him—which probably would have saved my hide—and I wasn't going to risk any more of my reputation defending him. I wasn't vengeful at that point; in fact, I felt badly that he had to endure what I'd been through, and more. His charges were serious—if the DOJ succeeded to the extent it hoped, Norris faced possible life imprisonment. Obviously, though, I would be of no use if I was going to implicate him in any criminal activity. I was safe because I wasn't involved—a bitter pill to swallow by that point.

The indictment and request for extradition was poignant. It was fueled by the 2003 United States/United Kingdom Extradition Treaty, primarily established to deal with terrorist issues after 9/11, but the U.S. government increasingly uses it for white-collar crime. It requires the DOJ to supply only an allegation of an offense instead of probable cause, which makes sense if you're trying to prevent an imminent terrorist attack, but its use for antitrust crime has many in the UK up in arms over what they perceive as the U.S. government's muscled, overreaching tactics.

Opponents hotly debate the issue, contending the treaty was signed without much parliamentary or public scrutiny, and they protest the issue of reciprocity. The U.S. requires evidence of probable cause in an extradition request, prompting some to label it a "one-way" policy and breach of human rights, authorizing "unrestricted kidnapping of British citizens

by U.S. prosecutors."[1] (In addition, the United States Senate hasn't rati-
fied the treaty, as of this writing). The controversy heated up in 2007
when British bankers, dubbed the "NatWest 3," were extradited to the
United States to face wire fraud charges in an Enron-related case. (They
accepted a plea deal and are awaiting sentencing.)

Norris's fast-track extradition case was the first one appealed and
finally tested in Britain's highest court, the House of Lords. As of this
writing, he won the first round of his battle. The United Kingdom passed
the Enterprise Act in 2002, which explicitly criminalizes price fixing, but
prior to that it wasn't illegal—he was indicted for activity that occurred
from 1989 to 2000, and Norris's attorneys successfully argued his actions
didn't violate a separate conspiracy to defraud offense under England
common law, either. A British newspaper quoted Norris after the victory:
"Even with the decision today, I still remain deeply concerned about the
one-sided extradition arrangements we have with the USA. It's a deeply
frightening situation to be in and I'm relieved that the UK justice system
has today stood up for its citizens."[2] The irony of that statement wasn't
lost on me. I was convinced my government would protect me when all
the facts came to light, but I wasn't so fortunate. I now realize convicting
me bolstered the case to get Norris.

The DOJ knows the best deterrent to antitrust activity is the very real
threat of being tried and imprisoned in the United States, and Norris's
partial victory surely had many other British businessmen breathing a
bit easier. If the DOJ was successful, it would have helped make the case
to extradite others accused of committing similar violations prior to
the Enterprise Act, including Sir Anthony Tennant, former chairman of
Christie's Auction House, whose American counterpart at Sotheby's, A.
Alfred Taubman, was convicted of price-fixing charges in 2001 and sent
to prison.

The DOJ clearly wants to send a message to foreign corporate executives who previously had little fear of violating antitrust laws. At an
international cartel conference in February 2007, Gerald Masoudi, Deputy
Assistant Attorney General of the DOJ Antitrust Division, cited Norris's
case as an example of international cooperation, saying, "Our efforts in
the Norris case should send a powerful signal that cartelists will not be

allowed to hide behind borders." The U.S. places foreign witnesses and subjects of investigation on border watches, or the Interpol Red Notice Watch, meaning fugitives run the risk of extradition if they leave their home countries. Many Norris supporters bemoan the heartbreaking manner in which he must at least initially spend hard-earned retirement years. It remains to be seen if Norris will ever be brought to the U.S. on obstruction of justice charges.

I was drawn to many of the claims made against Norris in the indictment that White and Case attached to their letter:[3]

"Defendant and his co-conspirators prepared a 'script' containing false material information which was to be followed by anyone questioned by either the Antitrust Division or the federal grand jury." *(That's what AUSA McClain asked about during our meeting in October 2003, but I never knew anything about a script. The Norris indictment said a U.S.-based employee had portions of it. Did Massaro have a copy in the files he was supposed to destroy?)*

"The conspirators removed, concealed, or destroyed from business files any documents which contained evidence of an anticompetitive agreement or reflected contact between or among competitors." *(I had zero knowledge that Massaro had any files of this nature or if he did, that he had destroyed them. When Norris told me Massaro was going to appear on the government's radar, I was alarmed, and I believe anyone would have asked Massaro the same questions I did.)*

Norris was concerned that certain employees would tell the truth about meetings they had with competitors. The indictment states that the "defendant implemented a plan to separate those employees from the company before they were questioned, either by placing them into retirement or making them consultants, so they could not be forced to testify in the investigation." *(That certainly explained Emerson's exit, but I instigated my early retirement myself, unknowingly sending the wrong signal to the DOJ.)*

Morgan Crucible assembled a task force to research files and remove, conceal, or destroy any documents or records reflecting a price fixing arrangement with competitors. *(I guess I unwillingly and unknowingly became part of that task force, but who were the people deliberately involved, and why weren't they prosecuted?)*

It was easy to see why White and Case wanted me as a defense witness. I was the one person who had gone to prison for the acts of others, and I couldn't make any incriminating statements against Ian Norris, other than he told me to tell "Tony and Laurence..." to take care of their files and that Massaro was going to appear on the government's radar. The letter from Norris's attorneys did give me the opportunity to contact AUSA Lucy McClain. I reiterated that when she and AUSA Rosenberg interviewed me at the Justice Department in September 2003, I had no knowledge of a cartel, price fixing in the United States or Europe, and no knowledge of any script or party line to follow if interviewed by the Justice Department.

My letter to McClain was based on the three questions I was asked at the December 2003, meeting:

> 1) Mr. Rosenberg: How do you explain that your prices on two families of parts at John Crane increased by 10 percent within two weeks of the January 29, 1997, meeting you attended in Toronto?
>
> *At the time Mr. Rosenberg asked question one, I was dumbfounded. I had no knowledge of any price increases at John Crane other than those associated with quantity changes. That statement covered ten years. During my tenure, there were only price reductions at John Crane. Unfortunately, I had to go to prison to find the answer to that question. I now have the answer, including the details of how it was done and who did it.*
>
> 2) Ms. McClain: We were told that all the global presidents were called to a meeting in London and given a script to follow. Did you do that?
>
> *As regards question two, I have never seen a "script." No one ever discussed a script with me or coached me in what to say to the Justice Department if I was ever interviewed. When I read the Justice Department's indictment of Ian Norris, I was shocked to see the lengths Norris and his co-conspirators went to cover up*

their crimes. Why do you think Norris wants me to testify on his behalf? I had no knowledge of what he was doing!

3) Ms. McClain: Will you help me prosecute Ian Norris?

Today, I believe I have information that will assist you and the Justice Department in the case against Norris while clarifying questions pertaining to me. I am willing to share that information which was obtained from Robin Emerson when we were both incarcerated at Eglin Federal Prison Camp.

Joe Tate has been in contact with [AUSA] Mr. Rosenberg about setting up a meeting for me to come to Philadelphia with Mr. J. David Quinn, who you have previously met. Some of the statements given me by Emerson were also given to Mr. Quinn when he visited me at Eglin. Emerson also confided in two other inmates telling them that I was an innocent victim. I have eight typewritten pages of names, dates, and details, some of which, I am confident you already have, but these details will only add validity to the information you don't have.

Ms. McClain, I cannot get back the three years this case took from my family and me. I cannot recapture the six months I spent in prison. I desire to bring finality and closure to this tragedy once and for all. I need to discuss this case with you in detail and I would like to do it now, not later.

Very truly yours,

F. Scott Brown

Dave Quinn once again accompanied me to the Justice Department Antitrust Division in Philadelphia in May 2005 for a meeting that lasted more than five hours. Assistant U.S. Attorneys Lucy McClain and Richard Rosenberg, and a new FBI agent were present. I had requested "Washington" be present, whoever that was, but there was no representative. We covered several areas of my case including Massaro's testimony to my investigator; my testimony regarding the Toronto meeting; Morgan

Crucible canceling my indemnification; Emerson's revelations; and the letter he sent me after prison. I was asked to provide copies of all relevant documents, which I did. During my presentation, Quinn told those present that Emerson had confided in him that I was an innocent man, as well as other information that Emerson had previously shared with me.

The meeting was open and cordial, but for me it was all business. When I finished my presentation, AUSA Rosenberg remarked that several people had testified against me. I agreed, but challenged him to look at the facts surrounding what actually took place at the Toronto meeting and the testimony provided the Justice Department by Klatt, Massaro, and Floyd.

Throughout the meeting, AUSA McClain was attentive and keenly interested. She asked me what else I thought could be done because my case was over.

"It isn't over for me. I'm considering writing a book about all this. I'm thinking about calling it *The Carbon Cartel—The Only American Standing.*" To my surprise, she encouraged me to write the book, and even offered to endorse a full pardon for me if I could get the paperwork to her desk.

She didn't have to ask twice, but when I returned home, I discovered I had to wait five years from my prison release date to even apply for a pardon. I wrote McClain and thanked her for her time, provided more historical documents that supported my version of events, and asked for any assistance she could offer regarding the pardon. I pointed out to her that the information I obtained from Robin Emerson was not available to me prior to entering my plea agreement. Dave Quinn's statements relative to my relationships with Ian Norris and Bill Macfarlane should have dispelled any notion that I was an insider at Morgan Crucible or that I participated in developing a script to obstruct justice.

My struggle still wasn't over, though. There was a second civil lawsuit filed against Morgan Crucible and Morganite that named me as a defendant—it was the final straw. The lawsuit accused me of fixing prices of electrical components sold in the United States. Since no one at Morgan Crucible was willing to stand up and state that I was never involved, I decided to take matters into my own hands and go on the offensive. I called Fred Wollman at his Raleigh, North Carolina office to express my displeasure with Morgan Crucible and how they were allowing my name to be drug through the mud.

Wollman responded by telling me he was sorry for not calling me earlier, but he was forced to make a decision: continuing our friendship or losing his job and his family's security. This was a sad conversation. If our roles were reversed, you can bet I would have stood up for what was right. This time, though, I was going to cooperate with the plaintiff's attorneys. Joe Tate represented me once again, this time pro bono, which I greatly appreciated because I decided not to have Morgan Crucible pay any more of my legal expenses.

The irony was mind-boggling: no current or former officer of Morganite or their U.S. manufacturing units were charged with price fixing or obstruction of justice. But I was, yet I had *nothing* to do with electrical products. And now here I was again, named in a civil lawsuit involving Morganite.

The attorneys for the plaintiffs came to Florida to meet with me, and picked me up at my home. I headed for the car, but Candy, who was understandably fed up with lawyers at this point, pulled them aside.

"My husband has been through enough," she firmly told them. "He's doing the right thing here, and I need assurance that you will do right by him. I cannot stand by and watch him go through any more pain." This was very out of character for my gentle wife, and the attorneys got her message loud and clear.

She and I didn't realize that God was using another challenging situation to grant us more enlightenment and comfort.

It is better to take refuge in the Lord than to trust in man.
—Psalm 118:8

Chapter 13

THE *EUROPEAN*
COMMISSION REPORT

T HE LAWYERS FROM THE FIRM CROWELL AND MORING AND I met in a private room at my golf club. For what seemed like the millionth time, I explained what I knew, and didn't know, about Morgan Crucible's antitrust activities. One of the attorneys kept flipping through a document and checking facts.

"What is that?" I asked. It was the *European Commission Report* (ECR). He handed it to me, and after scanning just a few pages, my blood pressure rose. "I need a copy of this," I said. He had one in my hands the next day.

The report, published by the Commission of European Communities (the European Union) on December 3, 2003, was a thorough investigation of the electrical and mechanical carbon and graphite industry cartel, and it was a bombshell in my eyes. It basically documented the involvement of each named company (there were six, including Morgan Crucible) in price fixing and other cartel activities, and, accordingly, how much each was fined. For me, it included most of the missing pieces needed to support my innocence.

As I read, I was both relieved and repulsed—the U.S. Department of Justice and Morgan Crucible's law firm, Sullivan and Cromwell, must have had a lot of the information in this report before I entered my plea and went to prison, but nobody told me or my attorney anything about it. Morgan Crucible paid no fines in Europe—zero—because it was the most forthcoming with documents and evidence about the cartel (authorities in Europe have legislation similar to the U.S. Corporate Leniency Policy with strong incentives—basically amnesty—for companies and individuals to cooperate with investigations). Sullivan and Cromwell supplied the Commission with extensive evidence and information that should have also been turned over to my lawyer based on our joint defense agreement, but it never happened! While I was mucking my way through false accusations, a rich, powerful company bargained in the stratosphere with European authorities and my own government.

The European Commission dealt with the companies based on the premise that tracking every violation is nearly impossible, so all the activity was treated as one "single continuous complex infringement."[1] Here are some key points from the somewhat technical and legalistic document:

The cartel dated as far back as 1937. The European Association of Carbon Brush Manufacturers, along with Morgan Crucible and Carbone Lorraine, established the Association of Manufacturers of Carbon Brushes, and an "agreement" to set minimum prices for customers in several European countries.[2]

Six companies participated during the timeframe under investigation by the European Commission, 1998–2000: Morgan Crucible, Conradty, Hoffman, Carbone Lorraine, Schunk, and SGL. Morgan Crucible, Schunk, and Carbone were also under investigation in the United States for antitrust activities for the same period.[3]

The Commission states that the general price increases in Europe were "discussed" and "agreed to" at "Technical Committee" meetings during the period 1988 to 1999. *(I didn't work for Morgan Crucible until 1995, yet I was the only American executive ever prosecuted.)*[4]

The "Technical Meetings" had to be compartmentalized between electrical, mechanical, and graphite products due to the number of different products and the complexity of the cartel's arrangements and activities, which changed over time. The purpose of the meetings is very clear: cartel member companies and their designees or representatives plotted to control the pricing of products they sold in various countries around the world, including the United States.[5]

Cartel members unified on pricing, surcharges to customers, leadership for certain major customers, a ban on advertising and participating at sales exhibitions, quantity restrictions for re-sellers or outright boycotts, and undercutting outside competitors.[6]

Cartel member companies met on a regular basis to insure the agreed upon pricing arrangements were maintained by the participating companies. The meetings were so numerous that each member company designated two people to contact to insure someone was available at all times.[7, 8]

Cartel members were supposed to agree on what to tell customers about price increases; for example, increases were necessary because of costs related to environmental regulations, wages, or inflation.[9]

The cartel had plans to deal with problem competitors: 1) lure them into cooperation, 2) pressure them into cooperation, 3) drive them out of business in a coordinated fashion, or at least teach them a serious lesson, or, 4) buy them. The report lists Pure Carbon's 1995 acquisition as an example of the cartel's strategies.[10]

At a 1993 cartel meeting, those in attendance stated, "Pure Carbon Company and its pricing policy is a major threat to all technical committee members." Pure Carbon's prices for standard products were between one-third and one-half that of cartel companies. Technical Committee members present at this meeting requested price increases of 15 to 20 percent for mechanical products, stating the actual prices are far too low compared to costs. *(Whose costs, theirs or Pure Carbon's? I was president of Pure Carbon Company in 1993, and our operating profit was significantly above standard for a manufacturing company. We were the low-cost manufacturer in the industry, and superior customer service was the catalyst for growth.)*[11]

When a competitor could not be bought, the cartel would take steps to disrupt the flow of materials to the competitor by purchasing the competitor's material source. Examples are SGL's purchase of Carbide Graphite Group located in St. Marys, Pennsylvania, and Morgan Crucible's purchase of Rekofa in Germany in 1998.[12]

The cartel companies met on a regular basis. Morgan Crucible adopted a special designation for representatives—The Club. The Commission Report describes elaborate precautions to conceal these meetings including gathering under the umbrella of the Association of European Graphite Electrode Producers and later the European Carbon and Graphite Association, and there were codes for individual companies; for example, Schunk was "G" for Giessen, Germany, and Morgan Crucible became "S" for Swansea. There was also a complicated system between member companies to compare and set pricing levels on products and parts. *(AUSA McClain once likened the activities of the carbon cartel to a well-controlled drug smuggling operation.)*

Schunk and Morgan Crucible agreed on price schemes for large customers. In 1998, Schunk placed a question mark next to the United States on a list of countries active in the cartel. *(This was a year after the Toronto meeting—the one where I supposedly set prices with Schunk. This is further evidence that Schunk was seeking price fixing coopera-tion from Morgan Crucible in the United States, but wasn't getting any help from me.)*[13]

Schunk and Morgan Crucible had special price schemes for some large customers like John Crane and Flexibox on mechanical carbon and graphite products. The pricing for those particular clients was regularly updated. *(I had zero knowledge or participation in the scheme.)*[14]

On October 13, 1998, cartel members formed a "Security Committee" to combat authorities in Europe and elsewhere who had instituted a series of actions against certain cartel members. Obviously, the initial actions of the Antitrust Division of the United States Justice Department had unnerved the French company Carbone, which turned over evidence to the DOJ about several carbon companies involved in cartel activities in the United States. Schunk later followed suit to avoid criminal prosecu-tion in the U.S. for their unlawful activities.

In 1999, some two years after the infamous Toronto meeting, Schunk and Morgan Crucible exchanged e-mails about price offers to John Crane, including market share (80–20 split), raising prices 4 to 5 percent, and limiting quotes to no more than twelve months. *(My efforts before and after these exchanges prove I wasn't involved in this scheme: I spent months negotiating the 1997 North American contract with John Crane that reduced prices 8 to 12 percent; at my direction, Morgan AM&T- The Americas invested more than $1.5 million in new equipment to lure John Crane's business; when I was global president in 2000, I signed a global purchasing agreement that reduced John Crane's prices another 7 percent, and there were no increases in Europe, including for Flexibox, which Crane owns.)*[15]

In November 2002, Morganite pleaded guilty in the United States to charges of cartel participation and price fixing on various types of electrical carbon products sold in the U.S., and parent company Morgan Crucible pleaded guilty to obstruction of justice. The fine was ten million dollars for cartel activity and one million dollars for obstruction of justice. *(The two global presidents who were highly involved in the electrical side and living in the United States were never prosecuted. It appears Morgan Crucible went to great lengths to protect these individuals since their testimony could possibly have tied Ian Norris, Bill Macfarlane, and others to price fixing and conspiracy to obstruct justice.)*

On September 24, 2003, four former executives of Morgan were indicted by a U.S. grand jury for influencing witnesses and destruction or concealment of documents in the period between April 1999 and August 2001. *(These were Ian Norris, Robin Emerson, Jack Kroef, former chairman of Morgan Crucible's Industrial and Traction Division, and me. All but Norris accepted a plea.)*

* * * *

The *European Commission Report* was incredibly enlightening and clarified the chaotic events that landed me in prison. I was intrigued by another finding. In Europe, the cartel members first used the Association of European Graphite Electrode Producers (AEGEP) to mask cartel meetings, and then the European Carbon and Graphite Association (ECGA) cloaked the get-togethers. Ian Norris resigned as Morgan Crucible's senior representative on the ECGA Board on March 1, 1999. That was near the time when it was disclosed that most of the ECGA members were being investigated for their involvement in the graphite cartel in both Europe and the United States.

It should be noted that several member companies of the National Electrical Manufacturers Association (NEMA) in the United States also dropped their memberships in NEMA at the same time, including Morganite, which withdrew following the completion of the chairman's term in office that year, who was the president of Morganite. On several occasions, NEMA executives solicited my help to encourage Morganite to rejoin NEMA. I discussed the request with Morganite's president and Norris several times to no avail. Morganite's president told me he felt NEMA provided no value to Morganite. Norris basically said it was Morganite's decision and wouldn't interfere, but encouraged me to continue as Morgan AM&T's representative; in other words, the mechanical carbon company in the United States remained a member of NEMA.

The year following Morganite's withdrawal, I was to become chairman of NEMA's Carbon Section. The day of the meeting, another member company asked me to step aside, and I refused, stating that I'd progressed through the chairs and it was my turn to head the Carbon Section. Later that day I was elected chairman. It's clear to me today that cartel members who attended NEMA meetings wanted their people to chair the section and control the agenda.

As chairman of the Carbon Section of NEMA, I made several significant changes. First, meetings that were previously held at resorts such as the Greenbriar, were moved to lower cost venues. Our first was in Orlando, Florida, and the cost for accommodations went form four hundred dollars per night to less than seventy. I also moved the spring meeting to NEMA's headquarters in Washington, DC, instead of a resort. During my time as chairman, member companies participated in a large-scale program to educate the academic world on the benefits of carbon for friction and wear applications inside the process stream of rotating equipment. We provided more than three hundred packets of information to major universities and colleges in the United States. I personally obtained literature from various participants and made all the mailings at Morgan AM&T's expense.

Again, events of the past were cast in a new light as I read the Commission report. The Commission investigation took years, and the DOJ likely had access to a lot of this information while I was being accused, threatened, and sent to prison. I simply cannot accept that the bulk of the ECR was not in the possession of the Justice Department while I endured accusations and ultimately prison. The deal had been struck and I was expendable.

The disclosure issue seriously carries over to Sullivan and Cromwell, Morgan Crucible's legal counsel. The ECR reads, "On 18 September 2001, Morgan met with the Commission to apply for leniency under

Commission Notice on the non-imposition or reduction of fines in cartel cases in respect of possible cartel activity in the European market for electrical and mechanical carbon products. On 5 October 2001, as agreed with the Commission, Morgan submitted the evidence available at the time. A supplementary submission of evidence was received on 30 October 2001."[16] Did Sullivan and Cromwell share this information with the United States Justice Department? Or were they simply turning over information to the European Union to avoid a large fine for Morgan Crucible and implicate other cartel members who had turned over evidence against Morgan Crucible in the United States?

This "cooperation" began two months after my subpoena. My attorney signed a joint defense agreement with Sullivan and Cromwell in January 2002, and I submitted to a lengthy interview with the attorney representing Morgan Crucible at the time, but we never received any of the evidence Sullivan and Cromwell handed over to the European Commission, which I question since we had a joint defense agreement. Where was Sullivan and Cromwell when I was being sent to prison? I believe I became part of Morgan Crucible's conspiracy—attention was diverted away from Morgan's electrical business and its management to mechanical carbon and me. I was the one person who could not finger Ian Norris or Bill Macfarlane at the time, and I had no knowledge of Tony Massaro's activities in the cartel until Robin Emerson disclosed those details to me at Eglin Federal Prison Camp.

When the U.S. government served its subpoena to Morgan Crucible in 1999, the company offered up a lot, including me, to avoid bigger fines, prosecution for the rest of its employees, and negative publicity. After twenty-seven months, why on earth would I suddenly become a prize worthy of a separate third-party subpoena while executives of Morganite and National Electrical Carbon, targets of the investigation in the first place, were let off the hook? When the investigation into the electrical carbon cartel started, mechanical carbon manufacturing supposedly surfaced as a problem—clearly somebody thought I'd be the fall guy. I don't know how Jim Floyd from Schunk and Tony Massaro from Morgan AM&T were pressured and manipulated during questioning, but something made them twist or fabricate facts in order to implicate me. (Robin

Emerson said the DOJ didn't ask certain questions about the Toronto meeting, so he never offered information about how I became angry and left the meeting before he, Klatt, Massaro, and Floyd sat down to exchange John Crane pricing documents.)

In one of Bruce Farmer's last actions as Chairman of Morgan Crucible, he made a reference in Morgan Crucible's 2002 Annual Report that a subsidiary of Morgan Crucible in the United States had been cited for illegal cartel activities. I found the statement to be a weak attempt at covering up a criminal corporate governance issue that had penetrated the boardroom of Morgan Crucible. Anyone who has read the *European Commission Report* knows that Morgan Crucible's involvement in cartel activities predates what occurred in the United States in 1998 and was obviously the forerunner for cartel activities after that time. Again, it appears Morgan Crucible wasn't accepting responsibility for its involvement.

It is also interesting to note that Richard Perle, well known in Republican circles in the United States and who served as United States Assistant Secretary of Defense from 1981 to 1987, became a non-executive director of Morgan Crucible in 1988. He resigned from the board of directors following the disclosure of the criminal issues facing Morgan Crucible in the United States. Today, Perle is resident fellow at the American Enterprise Institute in Washington DC.

On November 16, 2005, after I completed my study of the *European Commission Report*, I wrote AUSA McClain a seven-page letter that was thorough and vehement, stating especially:

> "It is my belief that Morgan Crucible took extreme measures to protect individuals involved in price fixing and a conspiracy in order to eliminate collateral damage their collective testimonies would have had both in the criminal and civil cases that followed."

I highlighted items in the report that supported both my assertions and Robin Emerson's revelations from Eglin. I referenced the *European Commission Report* as it related to my case:

- ECR: *Given the diversity of the price increases agreed (differing by country, type of product, and type of*

> *customer), it was inevitable that detailed notes were taken during technical meetings of the cartel, that is to say, at the levels of the technical committee and at local meetings. It was, however, an agreed rule, at least in later years, that no documents pertaining to the cartel should be kept in the company or even at home, but that they should be destroyed after having been implemented. Moreover, for the more strategic summit meetings, which ratified the price increases agreed at the level of the technical committee, participants strictly followed the rule of not keeping any notes, agendas, or reports at all. This rule was apparently strictly adhered to by participants, as the Commission has found only one written report of a Summit meeting, despite the existence of several leniency applications [exchanging evidence for prosecutorial and financial leniency].*[17]

I was told that Joseph Klatt had copious notes of meetings he had with me. Obviously that wasn't true, or he fabricated the notes after the fact. Klatt never made a note in my presence. The accuracy of his information was very poor.

"AUSA McClain, Joseph Klatt never discussed individual customers with me as he claimed happened at our second meeting near Giessen, Germany. He also covered up the fact that he made several threats to me at the Toronto meeting, as well as demands for splitting the John Crane resin bonded business and demanding 30 percent of the United States mechanical carbon market. He (Klatt) never received anything from me. We both know (now) that he exchanged pricing documents with Massaro after I left the Toronto meeting. Massaro, Jim Floyd, and Joseph Klatt failed to mention this to you, but Emerson's notes and his discussion with Mr. J. David Quinn have now been made part of the record."

- ECR: *"PIL" stands for Pure Industries, Ltd., a European subsidiary of Pure Carbon Corporation of the USA, which was taken over by Morgan in 1995.*[18]

"Prior to the takeover, Ian Norris told me there would be no changes in responsibilities. One week following the acquisition of Pure, Ian Norris phoned to say that it didn't make sense having me run PIL from the United States when Laurence Bryce was running Europe and living there. I was given South America instead and the cartel proceeded to put their "scheme" in place, assisted by Thein and Bryce, the two key mechanical carbon executives for Morgan AM&T–Europe (in 1995)."

- ECR: *An exchange of e-mails between Schunk and Morgan illustrates the close cooperation between the two companies in submitting price offers to a large OEM client, John Crane. On 7 January 1999, Schunk sent Morgan a list of carbon products for which John Crane requested price offers. The next day, Morgan e-mailed its reply to Schunk with the following message:*[19]

Having studied the detail on the lists I think we should consider the following points which we have discussed previously. If you are still in agreement with these we can proceed with the task of pricing the items accordingly:

Position prices to retain business share (80–20) at approx middle price.

Raise our base prices by 4 to 5 percent (single list for MAMAT).

No contract prices will be given for any item with an APU<4 (fifty per year).

We will not quote for more than twelve month quantities.

We will not give "next break" prices for less than 95 percent of total quantity.

We should request written contractual agreement stipulating that all un-shipped contract items will be taken within 1 month of the expiry of the contract period (or equivalent compensation paid).

All items will be quoted with a commercial lap finish only and if requested there will be a 5 percent surcharge for super-lapping.[20]

"The information contained in this paragraph is a smoking gun if ever I have seen one in this case. This information was obviously in the hands of Sullivan and Cromwell before I was sent to prison and before I entered my plea agreement. Once again, Sullivan and Cromwell has protected Morgan Crucible at the expense of Scott Brown. I sincerely believe, Ms. McClain, if you had the names of all the participants in this scheme, on January 7 and 8, 1999, it would have raised serious questions about the honesty, character, and reliability of those who testified against me. Again, for the record, I had zero knowledge of what these individuals were doing. I had no knowledge that our customer, John Crane, was ever treated unfairly.

This e-mail exchange is clear evidence that Morgan and Schunk, as well as several key management personnel, were clearly executing a scheme upon John Crane to allocate market share and set prices, terms, and conditions. It is my personal belief that the scheme failed twice. First, when I executed the North American agreement in March 1997, and, second, when I executed the global John Crane agreement nearly three years later on January 17, 2000. The agreement I signed on January 17, 2000, reduced prices significantly in the United States (7 percent) and Latin America (7 percent). There were no price increases in Europe, including Flexibox, or in the Asia-Pacific market. Schunk and Morgan (members of the cartel) wanted a 4 to 5 percent increase—yet they got nothing!

In addition, the John Crane contract I signed for North America in 1997 and was effective in March of that year resulted in price reductions of 8 to 12 percent. I believe I sent you a copy of this agreement following our May 11, 2005, meeting.

Once again, where were the Sullivan and Cromwell attorneys when I was being sent to prison?"

- ECR: *List of reported cartel meetings: 5 December 1996, Maidenhead, United Kingdom, Frederick's Hotel; local mechanical meeting.*[21]

"While the meeting may have been local, the subject was global; in other words, John Crane and Flexibox. The same parties referred to in the statements made by Robin Emerson while we were inmates at Eglin. Emerson's recollection of the discussions between Dr. Bruckmann, Joseph Klatt, Ian Norris, Edye Thein, Laurence Bryce, and Emerson were given to you on May 11, 2005. Most interesting is Emerson's comment that Schunk pushed for this meeting and the actions that followed. I believe this is further proof of the accuracy of Emerson's notes that John Crane and Flexibox were the subject of the meeting and setting of prices was the by-product."

In my letter, I reminded AUSA McClain that when we met in her office on May 11, 2005, AUSA Rosenberg remarked that several people testified against me. He was correct, but these were the same people whose names continually surfaced as participants and insiders who were heavily involved in cartel activities. Were they to be trusted? They got immunity. But Scott Brown went to prison.

In November 2005, I called AUSA McClain and asked her when she saw the *European Commission Report*. She said she couldn't disclose that information because the government was still involved with the Ian Norris case. This was another roadblock for me and my efforts to clear my name.

> Honest scales and balances are from the LORD; all the weights in the bag are of his making.
>
> —PROVERBS 16:11

One final comment I will make about AUSA McClain is that, even though we may not have agreed on everything, I will state in all candor that I personally respect and admire her. I believe she acted in good faith when I was prosecuted, given the information she had at that time. Unfortunately for me, that information came from those directly involved in cartel activities.

Chapter 14

LAWS OF GOD AND MEN

I SUPPOSE ALL THE PLAYERS WHO WERE ABLE TO ESCAPE PROS-ecution and leave this ordeal behind, as well as many outsiders, may view my six months in prison to be a small price to pay for the special consideration, or leniency, afforded Morgan Crucible and its employees. However, for my family and me this was about much more than those six months. The case consumed me for nearly six years, torpedoed my integrity and successful business reputation, turned me into a convicted felon, and caused health problems. I enthusiastically spent many years coaching youth sports and was involved in school programs—none of which I can do now because of the felony conviction; one small but significant way this ordeal unfairly altered my life. Of course there were many people, especially family and close friends, who pointedly told me to let go and move on, but those who know me best understood I would first protect my family from any more distress. I'm not the type to passively suffer injustice.

After my release I exchanged a few letters with Robert Osgood, Morgan Crucible's attorney at Sullivan and Cromwell, about the firm's total disregard of the joint defense agreement, which demonstrated very convoluted "legal ethics" surrounding disclosure. I told him that the time had come for others to account for their participation in activities that put me in prison for their actions.

This incredibly disheartening experience badly tarnished my patriotic view of America's judicial system. Early on, my attorney and friend Steve Salley presciently warned me, "Scott, the government is out to prove its case, and this will not necessarily be a search for the truth." At the time, still idealistic about my rights as a citizen and the honor of the American government, I rejected his pessimism.

My eyes have since been opened, but that doesn't mean I have to accept what I see—because I don't see justice. An astonishing aspect of the entire investigation is that several European cartel member companies acquired carbon businesses in the United States over the years, and these parent companies admitted guilt and paid substantial fines for antitrust activity, however they have been allowed to continue operating and making considerable profits in America. Why didn't the Justice Department force cartel members to divest their U.S. holdings? What sort of message does that send about breaking antitrust laws? What about the executives who were clearly involved in price-fixing activities and obstruction of justice, but got immunity from prosecution? I went to prison, but Morgan Crucible paid the minimum fine that can be assessed by the DOJ, and it pales in comparison to what other cartel members paid in Europe. (Morgan Crucible paid nothing in Europe because it came forward with so much information so quickly—it won the race to the courthouse.) Based on all the information I've gathered, I can draw no reasonable and prudent conclusion other than Joe Klatt, Jim Floyd, and Tony Massaro perjured themselves before the DOJ about what happened at the Toronto meeting in January 1997—and none of these men spent a day in jail or paid a single dollar in fines.

> A false witness will not go unpunished, and he who pours out lies will not go free.
>
> —PROVERBS 19:5

> Do not say, "I'll do to him as he has done to me; I'll pay that man back for what he did.
>
> —PROVERBS 24:29

(Revenge is often what the world seeks, but we must leave that in God's hands.)

When I stand back and look at the big picture, it does not look like justice. It looks like the U.S. government got most of what it wanted, and some of it came at my expense—that's my reward for being a law-abiding, hard-working citizen. How is this justice? I will never be convinced, especially in light of my clean record, that the charges against me warranted prison time instead of home confinement or parole, all permissible under a level-ten offense—even if I were guilty. And I was not.

As I mentioned at the beginning of this book, there really isn't a "secular" lesson in my experience. I did the right thing ethically and in all practical matters as far as my business career was concerned, but I went to prison. How depressing is that? Nobody can glean much guidance from that scenario. But the spiritual lesson sustained me as I was learning it.

Was I frustrated and consumed with anger sometimes? Yes. Were there times when I lost hope? Yes, but never completely. What I learned and now want to pass on to anyone reading or hearing about my story is that God is most present in those angry, hopeless moments if we reach out to Him. I thank God for my wife and the other people in my life who are firmly grounded in their faith and gave me the extra encouragement and hope I needed during very darkest days. I would never have made it through without God's hand lifting me up when I needed it most.

Candy reminded me of God's provisions throughout this incredible journey, one of which was the birth of our first grandson shortly after I was served my subpoena. Any grandparent can identify with the special joy of welcoming a first grandchild.

"His unconditional love was an amazing blessing at that time," Candy says. "When circumstances seemed suffocating, that little boy's affection gave you breath and peace." She is right. If there's one thing a helpless baby can do, it is remind you what's really important in life.

I decided to write this book not only for today, but for tomorrow. I have three young grandsons and a granddaughter now, and they need to know how God worked in their Granddad's life to reveal the truth about this case and emboldened me to persevere. I simply want to clear my name and reputation. And I also honestly and deeply love my country—I don't want anyone ever to have to endure an ordeal like mine. And I don't want my government misusing or failing to execute its judicial authority.

After my excruciating guilty plea before Judge Brody, she told me to use my experience to help others. Despite the outcome of my case, I respected Judge Brody's persistence in making sure I did the right thing that day. As disillusioned as I was about "blind justice" at that point, I realized she was personally committed to her responsibility to uphold the law.

Writing a memoir or just keeping a daily journal can be cathartic, helping an individual to clarify thoughts when putting feelings on paper (some of which should stay there). This was a complicated journey, and I had to document each painful step while it was fresh in my mind. The facts are black and white; I'm not seeking revenge nor have I attempted to maliciously disparage anyone. I have done nothing more than recount the verifiable facts of my case, and for which I possess exhaustive detailed proof from my six-year-long ordeal.

The truth is I was mad as hell when I started. But if I had not gone to prison, I wouldn't have discovered the key facts about my case from Robin Emerson. I mean, what are the chances that two Morgan Crucible employees serving prison sentences end up at the same place at the same time? God does not work by chance. If I hadn't been named in a second civil lawsuit, I wouldn't have found out about the *European Commission Report*, which documented the history of the cartel and Morgan Crucible's involvement. Again, it was all God's provision. He was in control, and I don't believe He delivered me from this ordeal so I could just silently walk away.

I have a small, inspiration picture of a man's hand holding the hand of a child on my desk at home. The caption reads, "Integrity, we make a living by what we get, we make a life by what we give." I believe those words and have always tried to live my life by giving my time, talents, and resources. I don't want my unfortunate experience to rob my family and me of the serenity that will allow us to continue living according to our foundational beliefs. I do want to move forward, but that doesn't mean I have to close my eyes to the past.

As I began writing this book in May 2005, I was determined to chronicle the events of my case as accurately as humanly possible. This book is a black-and-white account of what happened to me—there is no gray area! I have presented the facts of what occurred. My experience is a warning to others—it could happen to you.

As the months and years have passed since August 6, 2001, when I was first served my subpoena and subsequently sent to prison, "my story" has evolved to become what I believe is "God's story." God blessed me on this journey with revelations that have allowed me to unveil the truth behind the evil. Yes, God can and does use what man has intended as evil for His own good. In other words, "The light shines in the darkness" (John 1:5).

I am on a quest and pray God allows me to share this experience with business students, professionals, the legal community, and anyone who cares about business ethics and true justice in this country. I believe my story also offers hope and proof that God is gracious and the Source of all strength. It is my hope and fervent prayer that those who read this book will find wisdom and peace when faced with trials and tribulations in their lives.

God did not intend for us to live in a vacuum of self-centeredness, therefore it is my desire to share this experience and some of the important lessons I learned:

- Hold your company accountable. If I had any idea that Morgan Crucible participated in a cartel, I would never have supported or endorsed its acquisition of Pure Carbon. If you suspect management is involved in illegal activity, report it to proper authorities.

I tell you that men will have to give account on the day of judgment for every careless word they have spoken. For by your words...you will be condemned.
—Matthew 12:36–37

- Never be intimidated by your situation. We have a moral and ethical responsibility to do what is right. It doesn't take courage to win at any cost. God is your armor against falsehood and evil.

Be strong in the Lord and in his mighty power. Put on the full armor of God so that you can take your stand against the devil's schemes.
—Ephesians 6:10–11

- No legacy is as important as integrity. It's all or nothing— your integrity will be tested many times; don't turn it off when convenient. Your choices define you.

In everything set them an example by doing what is good. In your teaching show integrity, seriousness and soundness of speech that cannot be condemned, so that those who oppose you may be ashamed because they have nothing bad to say about us.

—Titus 2:7–8

- When your burden is heavy, the Lord will carry you; don't try doing it alone. It was only when I truly surrendered that my troubles were lifted.

Cast your cares on the Lord and he will sustain you; he will never let the righteous fall.

—Psalm 55:22

- Be mindful of those around you who work in secrecy and don't trust them. If they act like there's something to hide, there probably is. Be on guard for suspicious red flags.

It is better to take refuge in the LORD than to trust in man.

—Psalm 118:8

- The Lord can turn darkness into light. When troubles are out of your control, turn to the Lord. He used difficult trials to enlighten me, and I appreciated the revelations all the more.

Even in darkness light dawns for the upright, for the gracious and compassionate and righteous man.

—Psalm 112:4

- Rejoice in God's blessings, especially love. My family and friends supported me with unwavering love and prayers and never stopped believing in my innocence. I will forever thank God for this tremendous gift.

Love does not delight in evil but rejoices with the truth. It always protects, always trusts, always hopes, always perseveres. Love never fails.

—1 CORINTHIANS 13:6–8

- Finally, never forget how fortunate we are to live in the
  United States of America. I will not take freedom for
  granted again. Thousands have died for the rights we
  hold dear, and I believe we must all fight for justice—and
  against injustice.

We also rejoice in our sufferings, because we know that suffering
produces perseverance; perseverance, character; and character, hope.
And hope does not disappoint us, because God has poured out his
love into our hearts by the Holy Spirit, whom he has given us.

—ROMANS 5:3–5

* * * *

On Wednesday, October 15, 2008, I submitted my application to President Bush for a presidential pardon based upon the facts in this book.

You intended to harm me, but God intended it for good.

—GENESIS 50:20

APPENDIX OF PARTICIPANTS
AND PLAYERS

Jerry Bernstein, Attorney, Holland and Knight, New York

David Coker, Secretary to Board of Directors, Morgan Crucible

David Cooper, Global President, Morgan AM&T
    Former President, Morganite, Inc.

Robin Emerson, Employee, Morganite Electrical Carbon Ltd.

Dr. Bruce Farmer, Chairman, Morgan Crucible
    Former CEO, Morgan Crucible

James R. Floyd, Sales Manager, Schunk USA
    Former VP Silicon Carbide, Morgan AM&T
    Former Focus Accounts Manager, Morgan AM&T

Sutton Keany, Attorney, Pillsbury Winthrop

Joseph Klatt, Sales Executive, Schunk

Christine Levine, Attorney, Dechert Law

Bill Macfarlane, Member Board of Directors, Morgan Crucible
    Member Executive Committee, Morgan Crucible
    Chairman, Carbon Division, Morgan Crucible
    Former Chairman, Electrical Carbon Division
    Former VP/GM, National Electrical Carbon, USA

A. J. "Tony" Massaro, Vice President Sales, Morgan AM&T
    Former Vice President of Engineering, Morgan AM&T

Lucy P. McClain, Assistant United States Attorney, Antitrust Division

Scott Megregian, Attorney, Counsel to Schunk, for Schunk

Chandler Muller, Attorney, Counsel for F. Scott Brown, Winter Park,
    Florida

Ian Norris, CEO, Morgan Crucible
    Former Chairman, Carbon Division, Morgan Crucible

Robert Osgood, Attorney, Sullivan and Cromwell, (lead counsel, Morgan Crucible)

Sam Parkhill, President, The Stackpole Corporation

J. Dave Quinn, Member Global Board of Directors, Morgan AM&T
Former Member Board of Directors, Morgan AM&T–Americas
Former President, Pure Industries, Inc.
Former President, Pure Carbon Company

Cris Richard, Manager, Acquisitions and Divestures, Morgan Crucible

Richard Rosenberg, Assistant United States Attorney, Antitrust Division

Sam Seymour, Attorney, Sullivan and Cromwell (counsel, Morgan Crucible)

John W. Sharp, Jr.Agent, Federal Bureau of Investigation, Antitrust Division

Joe Tate, Attorney, Dechert Law, legal counsel for F. Scott Brown

NOTES

Foreword

1. James C. Collins, *Good to Great* (New York: Harper Business, 2001), 1.

2. Ibid.

3. Ibid.

4. William P. Young, *The Shack* (Newbury Park, CA: Windblown Media, 2007), 123–124.

5. Martin Luther, "A Mighty Fortress Is Our God," (1598).

Chapter 7
Arrows in the Dark

1. Taken from Department of Justice investigation documents, copies of which are in author's possession.

Chapter 8
Sensible but Searing Decisions

1. Web site: www.brainyquote.com/quotes/authors/m/martin_luther.html, accessed September 25, 2008.

2. Taken from Department of Justice investigation documents, copies of which are in author's possession.

3. Taken from Department of Justice investigation documents, copies of which are in author's possession.

Chapter 9
A Plea for Justice

1. Taken from transcript of sentencing hearing, copies of which are in author's possession.

Chapter 11
Unlikely Company

1. Taken from notes author kept during conversations with Emerson at Eglin Federal Prison.

2. *Merriam-Webster's Eleventh Collegiate* (Springfield, MA: Merriam-Webster, Incorporated).

3. Taken from Emerson's personal letter to Brown following Emerson's release from Eglin Federal Prison.

Chapter 12
True Freedom

1. From Web site www.lewrockwell.com/orig7/oliva4.html, accessed September 25, 2008.

2. "Extradition Victory for Ex-Morgan Crucible Boss," *The Independent*, from Web site: www.independent.co.uk/news/business/news/extradition-victory-for-exmorgan-crucible-boss-795056.html, accessed October 28, 2008.

3. Taken from the federal indictment documents, copies of which are in author's possession.

Chapter 13
The European Commission Report

1. European Commission Report, "13.3—Single and Continuous Infringement," p. 75.

2. Ibid., "5—The Origin of the Cartel," p. 20, (70).

3. Ibid., "1—Introduction," p. 2, (1).

4. Ibid., "6.1—Organisation of Contacts," p. 22, (76).

5. Ibid., "7.1—Prices, 7.11—Principles," p. 27, (91).

6. Ibid., "7.2—Surcharges, 7.2.1—Principles," p. 37 (111).

7. Ibid., "6.1— Organisation of Contacts," p. 22, (78).

8. Ibid., "7.1.2—Application," p. 31, (108).

9. Ibid., "7.1—Prices, 7.11—Principles," p. 27, (98).

10. Ibid., "7.9—Coordinated Attacks on Competitors, 7.9.1—Principles," p. 54, (167).

11. Ibid., "7.9—Coordinated Attacks on Competitors, 7.9.1—Principles," p. 54, (172), p. 56 (250).

12. Ibid., "7.8.2—Application," p. 54, (166).

13. Ibid., "7.1.2—Application," p. 31, (103).

14. Ibid., "7.6.2—Application," p. 43, (148).

15. Ibid., "7.6.2—Application," p. 43, (149).

16. Ibid., "2.2—The Commission's Investigation into the EEA Market for Electrical and Mechanical Carbon and Graphite Products," p. 16, (54).

17. Ibid., "6.3—Precautions to Conceal Meetings and Contacts," p. 24, (68).

18. Ibid., "7.6.2—Application," p. 49, (205).

19. Ibid., "7.6.2—Application," p. 49, (149).

20. Ibid., "7.6.2—Application," pp. 49–50, (149).

21. Ibid., "7.6.2—Application," p. 187, (Annex I, p. 114).

ABOUT THE AUTHOR

F. SCOTT BROWN IS THE FORMER PRESIDENT AND CEO OF Morgan AM&T, a wholly owned subsidiary of the Morgan Crucible Company. Morgan AM&T is a global supplier of pump seals and bearing components to the aircraft and aerospace, petrochemical, and general industrial markets. The company also manufactures personal body armor for the Department of Defense.

Brown's leadership of Morgan AM&T included thirty-nine manufacturing and sales locations around the globe. While employed by Morgan Crucible, Brown was a member of the Carbon Executive Committee of the corporation. Since 1974, Mr. Brown has been involved in various management and ownership positions in the carbon industry. Mr. Brown first joined the Pure Carbon Company in 1974 after having previously worked at the National Aeronautics and Space Administration (NASA) for ILC Industries in Houston, Texas.

In April 2001, Mr. Brown was inducted into the Legion of Honor by the J. Edward Kelley Society, formed after World War II to honor the memory of a young man who won the Congressional Medal of Honor and whose life was one of honor, integrity, and bravery.

In 1997, Brown was the recipient of the prestigious Pennsylvania American Legion Citizenship Award for his many contributions to the city of St. Marys and the state of Pennsylvania. In August 1999, Brown was inducted into the Pennsylvania American Legion Baseball Hall of Fame for his various contributions and support of baseball programs involving the youth of the state of Pennsylvania.

Brown has been actively involved in high school athletic programs for the better part of twenty-five years. In 1994, he became the head junior high football coach at St. Marys Area High School. In 1995, 1996, and 1997 he served as an assistant football coach at the same high school before becoming the head coach in 1998. Brown was a major organizer and contributor to the construction of Berwind Park, a state of the art American Legion baseball field in St. Marys, Pennsylvania and was one of the three individuals responsible for the construction of the girl's softball facility at St. Marys Area High School.

While a resident of St. Marys, Pennsylvania, Brown was a member of the Board of Directors of the St. Marys Regional Hospital, a member of the Board of Directors of the DuBois Foundation of Pennsylvania State University, a member of the Board of Directors of the Dickinson Mental Health System, President of Post 103 American Legion Baseball, a member of the Executive Committee of the Boy Scouts of America, and a member of the Scouting Heritage Society. Mr. Brown is a former founder and Director of the St. Marys Community Education Council, and a former Director of the St. Marys School District's Schools-to-Work Program.

Brown is a former Board member of Nova Manufacturing in Nova, Ohio, National Specialty Products in Findley, Ohio, and Morris Compressor of Houston, Texas.

Brown is currently an active member of St. Peter's Episcopal Church in Lake Mary, Florida, where he has served as Co-chairman of the Capital Campaign to build a new sanctuary. Mr. Brown is an active member of the Grace-n-Grits outreach ministry of Sanford, Florida, which serves the less fortunate of the area on a weekly basis.

Mr. Brown has been a member of Lodge 273 A. F. & A. M. for the past forty-three years. He is also a member of the Coudersport Ancient and Accepted Scottish Rite.

Mr. Brown earned his Master of Business Administration degree from California Western University and wrote his thesis on "The Development of a Marketing Support Program for New Industrial Products." In addition, Mr. Brown has completed executive management courses at North Carolina State University, Babson College, and San Jacinto College.

Scott and his wife, Candy, have been married for thirty-eight years and have three grown children and four grandchildren.

TO CONTACT THE AUTHOR

Attention: F. Scott Brown

Out of the Valley, LLC.

P.O. Box 951419

Lake Mary, FL 32795

or

fscottbrown@bellsouth.net